THE
BAFFLED PARENT'S

GUIDE TO

Stopping
Bad
Behavior

THE BAFFLED PARENT'S GUIDE TO

Stopping Bad Behavior

KATE KELLY

Contemporary Books

Chicago New York San Francisco Lisbon London Madrid Mexico City
Milan New Delhi San Juan Seoul Singapore Sydney Toronto

Library of Congress Cataloging-in-Publication Data

Kelly, Kate.
        The baffled parent's guide to stopping bad behavior / Kate Kelly.
                p.   cm.
        Includes bibliographical references.
        ISBN 0-07-141169-0
        1. Discipline of children.   2. Child rearing.   3. Parenting.   4. Parent
and child.   I. Title.

HQ770.4.K45   2003
649'.64—dc21   2002041488

1 2 3 4 5 6 7 8 9 0   AGM/AGM   2 1 0 9 8 7 6 5 4 3

ISBN 0-07-141169-0

Interior design by Think Design Group

McGraw-Hill books are available at special quantity discounts to use as premiums and
sales promotions, or for use in corporate training programs. For more information, please
write to the Director of Special Sales, Professional Publishing, McGraw-Hill, Two Penn
Plaza, New York, NY 10121-2298. Or contact your local bookstore.

This book is printed on acid-free paper.

Contents

Acknowledgments

Thank you to all the parents, teachers, and professionals who shared information, advice, and anecdotal experience for the benefit of this book. A special thanks to Kathryn Whipple, who provided invaluable help in conducting research on this very important topic.

Lessons from a Parent

Like most parents, my husband and I learned about stopping bad behavior in our children by the seat of our pants. We drew upon our own backgrounds and advice from parents, the pediatrician, and our friends, and we worked heavily from instinct. Overall, our daughters, their teachers, and our own parents would give us pretty good marks on our progress thus far. Still, I jumped at the chance to more closely evaluate the process of stopping bad behavior. Researching and writing this book has been a wonderful opportunity to take a look at what experts in the field have to say on the topic.

As I read and listened to teachers, parents, and psychologists tell about stopping bad behavior, I thought particularly about three specific instances in my own parenting experience. Each of these personal experiences illustrates some of the important principles of helping kids learn to behave well. As it happens, each of these instances involves a different daughter, supporting the idea that you learn something new with each child. Let me share with you a little of what I've learned.

The Power of Consistency

With my firstborn, we lived in a city and I worked early in the day, so we would frequently meet friends at a nearby playground in the late afternoon. Playgrounds are one of those places where most parents and children begin to feel the generational divide. While children can stay at a playground indefinitely, most parents reach a breaking point where they get tired, need to get to the grocery store or fix dinner, or just plain would rather go home. When my daughter was a toddler and began moving around the playground under her own volition, I quickly learned that we had to have a system that would permit me to take control at a certain time. I chose the old "three more times" technique (three more times on the slide, three more times balancing across the little wall, etc.), and instinctively, I *always* made her stop after the third time. Countless times when we were with friends, I watched as another mother would offer a similar rule and then continue her conversation while her child went up the monkey bars five, ten, or fifteen more times before she eventually pulled the child off the bars for the journey home.

Not until my first daughter became an adolescent did I realize how important it was that I stuck by what I said. I listened to friends whose children were young adolescents. The kids argued back about curfews or didn't call when they said they would, and many, many issues seemed, to the kids anyway, to be negotiable.

Little did I know at the time how important those "three more times" days at the playground were for laying the groundwork of our relationship: When I make a deal with any of my daughters (whether it's three more times on the slide or being home by 11:00 P.M.), we stick to it. So from Daughter Number One I learned the power of consistency. (I also know that consistency is important both ways. If I promise her something, I make sure I live up to it, just as I expect her to do for me.)

Parenting with Sensitivity

With Daughter Number Two, I learned that good behavior should always be the expectation, but sometimes your children can teach you how to set the terms. When my second daughter was about two years old, I was scheduled to give a speech about being a writer to a paying audience of about a hundred people in my hometown. The kids had gone on the trip with me, and I'd hired a local teenager to take care of the children, then almost six and two, in a room down the hall from where the luncheon was taking place. A few minutes into my remarks, everyone in the room heard loud wails in the hall, and my two-year-old burst into the room and ran directly to the podium, wrapping herself around my leg. Instinct kicked in. Separation anxiety was a big issue for this daughter, and I knew I would never successfully peel her off my leg in such a way that I could continue my remarks with any dignity. I also knew that I could "stop her bad behavior" by solving her problem: she wanted me. I picked her up and gave the rest of the speech with her in my arms, and she didn't wiggle, yank at the microphone, or make a peep. Her behavior couldn't have been better.

After the speech, a mother in the audience approached me and told me how she handles it when her children want her attention and she's busy. "If I'm reading, I keep a washcloth and a bowl of cold water near me. If they come and want something, I wash their face with the icy cold water, and they go away."

What a contrast in lessons the two of us were teaching. My method involved high standards but with flexibility. My kids learned that if they need me, I'm available to them. That, too, has been oh, so important as they've been growing up. What do you suppose the children greeted with ice water have done through the years if they've had a tough problem? I'll bet they haven't turned to their mothers. What do you think?

Keep Them Safe at All Costs

My third daughter surprised me the most, for she taught me a lesson I thought I would never have to learn about the lengths you may have to go to in order to keep a child safe. Daughter Number Three spent her womb time exercising her legs as often and as hard as possible. I should have suspected she would be an active one, and she certainly was. I tell her—and it isn't far from the truth—that I spent the first four years of her life running after her, through yards and parks and shopping malls and around restaurants. One day when she was about four and a half, she stopped and held my hand, and I couldn't have been more surprised.

If you have a child like this—and they are quite common—then you know that your biggest issue has to do with keeping him or her safe. Often I would be distracted by a remark from one of my older girls or a kick of a soccer ball at one of their games, and the next thing I knew,

Callie would be off on some new adventure—twelve to fifteen feet ahead of me. After years of condemning people who use harnesses on their children, I finally understood—I needed a way to keep her safe. We started off with what I deemed the more socially acceptable kind, where a Velcro piece wraps around the child's wrist. She unfastened it on day one. We then had to resort to the far less socially acceptable style—the zip-on harness (hers was a lovely pink).

If I could focus 100 percent on Callie, I would let her run free, but when I was in an airport, a store (where she could run beneath clothing displays where I couldn't find her), or at one of her sisters' sporting events, we zipped on a harness. I would follow where she led as much as possible so as not to frustrate her, but I no longer had to worry about literally losing her and seeing her harmed.

So from Callie I learned that sometimes the parent just has to be the boss. There are certain behavioral issues that children are not capable of understanding. There comes a time when you simply have to take over and be the parent they deserve to have you be.

As for Callie, is her spirit broken? Is her love of freedom dimmed? Not at all. While we are only beginning the teen years, those who know her will testify that *energetic* and *exuberant* are two words that still fit her best.

Why This Book Is Important Both Today and Tomorrow

The Baffled Parent's Guides are planned and written to focus on the how-tos of parenting. You don't have to get bogged down reading the whys of a tantrum; you can get to the heart of the matter and find out *what to do* during the tantrum. You'll find the answers you're looking for, organized so that you can find topics quickly and easily.

The behavioral lessons I've just shared with you (be consistent; parent with sensitivity; keep them safe at all costs) are representative of what you'll learn as you read this book. These lessons apply to managing children of any age. The parenting skills you are developing and the groundwork you are laying today are going to last a lifetime. These methods will serve you well from the first play date right through to the prom.

Making your four-year-old help put away the blocks or expecting your nine-year-old to remember to call you at a certain time may seem like small potatoes compared with many other issues. However, the style and expectations you set today will follow you into the turbulent years of adolescence and beyond.

You love this little kid who may sometimes give you a tough time. Love her enough to work hard at establishing behavior that makes her pleasant to have around now and for the rest of both your lifetimes.

Parenting is a lot of work, but the rewards make the worry and effort worthwhile. Enjoy.

PART ONE

No Family Is Perfect All of the Time

CHAPTER 1

All Parents Are Baffled Some of the Time

*M*ark and his twin sister, Maria, are model children. They go to bed on time, get up without being cajoled, get dressed promptly, and at age seven, come downstairs to help prepare their own breakfasts. After eating, they brush their teeth (without being reminded), pick up their prepacked backpacks, and skip down the front walk to meet the school bus. Sounds like the parents in Mark and Maria's household have a pretty easy time, doesn't it?

While you might like to have an occasional morning like this in your household, we all know that achieving the kind of "perfection" described here would be extraordinarily difficult. Like adults, even the best-behaved children slip up, forget things, wake up feeling grouchy, and sometimes just don't feel like cooperating—because they are human.

All families are probably very much like your own. Dad is running out the door, hoping he can make up the few minutes he lost having to clean up the cereal four-year-old Susie accidentally spilled when carrying her breakfast bowl to the table. Susie has finally quieted down after bursting into tears when Dad exploded over the spill. Mom is hurrying nine-year-old Tom along as he sleepily gathers last night's homework and literally stuffs it into his backpack before coming down for breakfast. Two-year-old Timmy is standing, fists clutched around the bars of his crib, screaming, "MommEEEEE! Get up now!!!! Timmy get up now!!!" Mom, half-dressed for work, rushes in to say a comforting, "Two min-

Did You Know?

Maybe some of our children's issues could be solved by letting kids be kids. A new study from the University of Michigan found that playing gets only 25 percent of a child's free time today, in contrast to 41 percent in 1981.

utes, Timmy. Just two minutes. Let me get my shoes and stockings on, and then I'll take you down to breakfast."

This family is a totally normal, loving family who may sometimes need a little help. While this morning's problems mainly have to do with the chaos that is already coloring the beginning of the day, Susie, Tom, and Timmy have been known to whine, talk back now and then, have tantrums, and generally "misbehave" in the way all kids do. Guess what—they are totally normal.

I want you to understand right now that this book is in no way about creating "perfect" children—you don't even *want* Mark and Maria living in your house. This book is about helping parents like you who love your children wildly, enjoy being with them, love the life and vigor children have brought into your home—but would still like to know what to do when your son openly insults Grandma's cooking, your daughter pulls several shenanigans to avoid going to bed on time, and your toddler has an extremely vocal tantrum in the grocery store because you refuse to buy him a box of Crunchy Cap'n Choco-cereal.

The Baffled Parent's Guide to Stopping Bad Behavior is about helping normal families find ways to make family life as pleasurable as possible. It shows how to correct bad behavior and create new patterns where annoying behavior has become a set response to a particular situation (such as when your toddler always throws a tantrum when it's time to leave Grandma's house). Most important, this book tells you how to create an atmosphere that encourages good behavior, so that you have to deal with stopping bad behavior fewer and fewer times.

The Validity of Your Goals

While your first goal almost certainly has to do with bringing down the frustration, anger, and annoyance in your household, there is a second, more important goal that provides you with the reason why you absolutely must fight to stop your children's bad behavior. The broader purpose of stopping bad behavior—disciplining your children—has to do with creating upstanding citizens who know how to take care of themselves but are sensitive to the world around them.

Great Idea!

One teacher tells how sometimes you have to think outside the box:

"One morning, I had a lot of ground to cover, and I could barely get through attendance. I stopped midway and softly began singing the school song, inviting my students to join in. A few students stopped briefly, then went back to playing. When I stopped and began rattling off the first assignment, they stopped and said they would sing but asked me to leave the room. I waited in the hall for about ten minutes. When I came back in, the students were standing beside their desks, the lyrics were on the board, one student was cheerleading, another using the desk as a drum, and another beatboxing. They sang beautifully and in unison. They were proud and could see how proud I was to have such a creative class. Sometimes you have to veer off course and allow your classes to flow."

From the day your baby is born, you are working to achieve a goal that may take eighteen, twenty-one, or even twenty-five or more years to accomplish. You're trying to work yourself out of a job by instilling in your child self-mastery for the day your child will be fully responsible and in charge of himself. Many issues that involve keeping your child safe—such as teaching a child not to touch a hot stove or how to cross a street properly—will be accomplished in just a few years. Issues such as promptness and self-discipline take much longer to instill. (By the age of eighteen, does she have the self-discipline to get up with the alarm to get to an 8:00 A.M. college class? Does he have the self-mastery at thirty to work in advance on the marketing report that is due next week?)

Children who are raised with the correct balance of freedom and discipline become people who can enjoy all the pleasures of life. They know how to take care of themselves, they recognize the benefits of social niceties, and they understand how others feel, so they can adjust their behavior as needed when unexpected or unusual occasions arise. Ultimately, you've done a good job because you have successfully taught them how to parent themselves.

At Wit's End

*"The thing that impresses
me the most about
America is the way
parents obey their
children."*

—King Edward VIII

The Value of Parental Agreement

Parents who present a united front on discipline have the best results. Discuss with each other your feelings about stopping bad behavior. Discipline issues bring up strong emotions in all of us, and by talking together parents can develop a unified plan on how to approach certain behavior issues. In general, an ideal system involves letting the parent who is with the child at the time of misbehavior handle it as he or she sees fit. The days of "wait until your father gets home" should be long gone—such statements establish Dad as the "bad guy," and the threat creates undue anxiety for a child who would have been better off with an immediate response such as, "I told you not to hit your brother, and you hit him again. You'll have to come and sit in the kitchen with me, and let him watch TV in peace."

If you are divorced, discipline takes on new complexity. You can double the hassle factor if there is a stepparent and/or stepchildren who live with you some or most of the time. (Then you have your ex and your spouse's ex whose attitudes also have to be factored into yours and your new spouse's discipline practices.) While children can certainly learn to understand that rules are different in Mom's house and Dad's house, it is helpful if all adults come to some basic agreement on the way to handle discipline issues such as tantrums, hitting, or sassing. Whether or not a child is expected to make his or her bed at one house and not at another is less important than the permissibility of specific negative behaviors such a those listed above.

Obstacles to Teaching Our Children Good Behavior

Why are these behavior issues so difficult for parents? It's not particularly hard to plan a meal for a family, play a game with a child, or even to put most babies to bed. What is it about bad behavior that makes it so difficult to manage?

To begin, for most people, *discipline* has a negative connotation. We all expect to give birth to a Mark or a Maria who is just "perfect" because he or she is ours. When we fall in love with these wonderful beings we tend to overlook their imperfections.

Then suddenly from his crib Mark throws a toy at Dad's head, and Maria starts shrieking when Aunt Sylvia attempts to pick her up. What's going on here? Suddenly parenting isn't so much fun anymore. You can't send Mark to his room for throwing the toy, because he's already in his room. And who do you deal with first—Aunt Sylvia, who has become quite frosty to everyone because of Maria's reaction, or Maria, whom you can't quiet down?

There's also the perplexing issue of *how* to discipline. Does anyone spank anymore? Can I send a toddler to his room to learn a lesson? You know the ten-and-under set is too young to be grounded, but when are they old enough for a stern talking-to? And what's with time-outs? Do they work?

"Wait a minute," you say. "I'm not prepared for this!"

None of us are. But there are valid reasons for our lack of preparation, and understanding those reasons actually makes us more prepared.

At Wit's End

"Raising kids is part joy and part guerrilla warfare."

—Ed Asner

Why Stopping Bad Behavior Is So Complicated

Stopping bad behavior in our children is perhaps one of the most difficult aspects of parenting because every single one of us is mired in layer upon layer of very strong feelings about the issue. The following list describes some of the most widespread feelings:

- *Rejection of how we ourselves were raised*—You may have strong and negative memories of how you were disciplined (spanking? being sent to your room? all the siblings being punished if one did something wrong?). As a result, you may intend to avoid those methods at all costs. Or you may have been raised in a very relaxed household and eventually realized that it would have been easier if a parent had provided some disciplinary guidelines.
- *Desire to replicate some of the systems used as you were growing up, and frustration that times are different*—Maybe there are a lot of things you think your mom and dad did correctly, and you intend to

implement them with your own children. However, if big family dinners were one of the ways your parents kept a firm hand on the family, you may have difficulty copying that tradition in this hectic day and age.

- *Differences in parenting styles and beliefs*—Your spouse may believe strongly in one form of discipline—one that is exactly opposite to what you believe. When such disagreements emerge, emotions between the two of you may be running high, even before your child does something you disapprove of. As previously mentioned, the situation gets more complicated when ex-spouses and stepparents are involved. These issues need to be worked out before misbehavior occurs.

- *Reactions from adults around us when we're stopping bad behavior*—Whether it's your mother-in-law, the day-care teacher, or the lady in the grocery store who witnesses how you handle your four-year-old's tantrum, we tend to feel self-conscious when all eyes are upon us. (And if your child is creating a huge scene, then you probably *are* being closely and judgmentally observed!) Unfortunately, many people don't hesitate to comment on what they think would work better. Whether these well-meaning individuals are in-laws, friends, or strangers, their interference affects us.

- *The child's personality*—It isn't that we love one child more than the other or favor a particular child, but it is true that we parent each child differently. Your attitude may be determined by your feelings about each child's style of behavior. Perhaps your devilish four-year-old thinks of annoying—but funny—things to do, and you can't help but chuckle some of the time. Or you may be going through a phase when the whining of one of your kids is like fingernails on a chalkboard, so you may be more prone to get angry with her. Or your behavior may be dictated by birth order—both yours and your child's. If you are a firstborn yourself, you may identify strongly with your own first child and be more sympathetic to the plight she faces as leader of the siblings.

- *Knowing when to let things slide*—The ten-month-old who finds it amusing to throw things off the high chair tray soon grows into an eighteen-month-old who is old enough to know better. The challenge for parents is learning when to encourage higher standards. Remember that the five-year-old who is "too young" to do chores will eventually become an eight-year-old who is plenty old enough to help out around the house.

- *Concern about attitudes of society*—"Back when I was growing up . . ." takes on new meaning when you become a parent. Times have changed, and society has become more lax—less formal—about many issues, such as what we wear to church or temple services. Few people would agree with our grandparents that "children should be seen more than they are heard." We find that change has occurred in parenting issues. Nursery school teachers tell tales of parents deferring to their preschoolers for opinions on issues that these youngsters are far too young to evaluate. A mother will actually consult her three-year-old about whether he will be too tired after nursery school to take karate. While there are many valid reasons to avoid responding to all issues with, "You'll do it because I say so," there's something to be said for the parent who can step forward and take responsibility for being the parent. Now and then a firm, "We're doing it this way because I'm the parent," isn't such a bad thing.

- *Anger, even rage, in the heat of the moment*—It is the rare parent who can listen to backseat whining throughout a thirty-minute car ride or dispassionately watch her child call a lady in an elevator "a big fat poop" without reacting emotionally. None of us are at our best when we are angry. While there are occasions when outright indignation or anger is effective with a child, most of the time, the best way to stop bad behavior is to handle it calmly.

If you feel perplexed about how to discipline your child and your stomach knots up sometimes when you realize that things really have gotten out of hand, this list explains why. You're simply normal.

Let's get started right away. In Chapter 2, you'll read about ways to set the scene for improving your children's behavior.

At Wit's End

"There was a time when we expected nothing of our children but obedience, as opposed to the present, when we expect everything of them but obedience."

—Anatole Broyard, author

CHAPTER 2

Inspiring Good Behavior

*Fourteen Simple Practices That
Make Parenting Easy*

"Ah, now we come to the discipline part of the book," you may be thinking.

The answer is, "Not really." Regardless of the true meaning of discipline, we tend to think of it as a no-questions-asked method of enforcing our will on our children. Stopping bad behavior has more to do with guiding your child than it has to do with disciplining him or her. Guiding toward good behavior is very effective, less stressful for both parent and child, and a heck of a lot more fun.

Smiles, Not Storm Clouds

Children at all ages would prefer to bring smiles to your face rather than storm clouds. However, the entire behavioral process is about self-control: the ability to make choices about how to behave, instead of responding to impulses. Self-control is very difficult for young children to learn. As children learn this (a process that can take a long time), they will be able to consider the consequences of acting on their first impulse—simply put, to think before acting.

It is the parents' job to guide and aid in this self-mastery. As you do so, you'll find that your children generally want to behave well. When

At Wit's End

"The best inheritance a parent can give to his children is a few minutes of [his or her] time each day."

—M. Grundler, writer

11

they lose control, they will actually appreciate it when you rescue them from their misbehavior or rage.

A major cause of bad behavior is feeling out of control, a feeling that is often stimulated by heightened frustration. Unfortunately, frustration occurs frequently throughout childhood, as kids try to master so many different things. We can make some general observations about children who have achieved a feeling of control:

- They have learned about the common rules that dictate society (no shoving, no cursing, no hitting, and so on).
- They have been given some choice over their lives. (Would you like to wear the blue shirt or the red one?)
- They have some responsibility for themselves and, later, for the work-ings of the family. The toddler who learns to put on his own shirt, the preschooler who is responsible for setting the table, and the nine-year-old who walks the dog are all achieving a positive self-image as peo-ple who can do good things.
- They are learning impulse control. Just as adults know not to tell the boss what they really think of him, children need to learn not to act on everything they think of doing or saying. That's part of civilized living. Not acting on impulse also helps keep children safe. They learn not to follow the ball into the street without looking or to wan-der far from home.
- They are learning age-appropriate problem solving. When your child wants to use a shovel in the sandbox, she doesn't just hit the friend who is playing with it. Instead, she learns to use words to ask for a turn.
- They have been exposed to the values that are important to their fam-ily and community. Whether it's kindness to animals or the concept that it hurts a friend's feelings if you don't include him in the game at recess, children are ready recipients of the values you think are important.

While Parts Two and Three of this book are filled with specific advice to guide your child's behavior, this chapter is devoted to fourteen simple principles that can make a world of difference.

Principle 1: Set a Good Example

The most powerful learning tool children have is absorbing and imitating what they see around them, so parents, older siblings, teachers, and caregivers have an enormous impact on a child's behavior. Whether you're aware of it or not, your children watch you constantly, absorbing the way you handle frustration, your behavior when you're angry, your level of honesty, your reaction to new people and events, and your response when you're pleased about something.

Part of becoming a parent involves reevaluating some of our own activities. Just as women smokers try to quit before becoming pregnant, parents may want to work on various behaviors in order to set a good example for their kids. Certainly, how you handle stress and anger are important issues to consider, as managing these issues is critical for human beings of all ages.

Part of being a good role model also involves sometimes explaining what you do. "I'm calling Grandma today to see how she's feeling," or, "I'm sorry I'm not listening very well. I had a hard day at work."

One of the greatest lessons you can model for your child is the ability to apologize. If you yell at your child with little provocation, bang pans around in the kitchen because you had a bad day at work, or are just out of sorts one day, saying, "I'm sorry I yelled at you," or, "I'm sorry I'm so grumpy today," will mend almost any wrong. On a far higher plane, you'll be teaching your child that everyone makes mistakes, but they can be remedied by a heartfelt apology.

Principle 2: Encourage Competence

You love your child and enjoy watching her learn and do so many things. As a baby, she crawls and eventually takes early steps; the toddler learns to ask for something nicely; the three-year-old brings you a "prezzy" of a drawing from school; the four-year-old teaches his little sister to moo; the five-year-old learns to skip; and the elementary school child acquires a long list of school-related accomplishments. The progress your child makes each day is enormous. The child who finds it easiest to be well-

At Wit's End

"Few things are harder to put up with than a good example."

—Mark Twain

Great Idea!

Remember that change doesn't come overnight for children or adults.

behaved is one who has been praised for daily milestones. For children of all ages, psychologists often tell parents, "Catch them being good," and comment on it. Parental attention followed by honest praise (not unnecessary compliments) will take both you and your child a long way on the road to good behavior.

Self-confidence is a good stepping-stone on the way to self-control.

Principle 3: Teach Social Skills

While we no longer believe in social mores such as "children should be seen and not heard" and many adults no longer care about being addressed as Mr. or Mrs., when it comes to manners, it's important not to throw the baby out with the bathwater. The well-behaved child gets along with other children and adults, because he respects the rights of others and understands the importance of a certain level of social order. If Ann is already waiting to talk to the teacher when Nick comes to the desk, it's important for Nick to understand he must wait. Manners put people at ease and enable them to live and work together more smoothly.

Toddlers can learn "please" and "thank you." Eventually they can learn not to interrupt and can understand the words *you need to wait for just a minute*. Even a three-year-old can begin to observe and practice the art of meeting a new acquaintance (look a person directly in the eye, extend a hand to be shaken, and say, "I'm pleased to meet you"). While three may seem early, remember children are going to react to a new person somehow. Early social skills are far preferable to pulling on your arm, hiding behind your leg, or whimpering, "Mommy, mommy, mommy," out of nervous reaction to someone new. Phone skills also can begin early, as it is a very happy toddler who receives permission to answer the phone.

As children get a little older, you can introduce expectations for taking turns, standing in line, and asking permission. Experiences with your child in the car, in the grocery, at a restaurant, at a movie, and on a plane are all times to introduce proper behavior.

Look at these early lessons as a favor you do your children. The business executive who has never been taught proper table etiquette is at a serious disadvantage when it comes to being promoted. Teach your children these skills now so that they won't be at a disadvantage later on.

Principle 4: Give Children an Age-Appropriate Amount of Control

Successful parenting involves navigating the difficult line between too much and too little independence. Often we want to give our children the autonomy they are struggling for. At the same time, parents have to understand that it's important for children to leave the house on time or come home from the playground before it's dark. At those times a parent must often take control.

Simple decisions can do a great deal to help you find this delicate balance. Saying, "Lisa, go pick out what you want to wear tomorrow," may result in Lisa wanting to wear her bathing suit in January. Instead, say, "Lisa, do you want to wear your blue striped shirt or your red one?"

Decisions should be scaled to the age of the child and offered as often as possible. Parents who help build this kind of decision-making skill will find positive short-term and long-term results. The child who has had a say in what she's wearing to school the next day will be more cooperative about getting dressed and will eventually be capable of laying out her own clothing for a weekend at Grandma's.

With privilege (the privilege being some control) comes responsibility. If Josh can dress himself and be ready for preschool by the time you've established, then he can dress himself. If he tends to get distracted and can't get it together in the morning, then you'll have to help him get dressed. Over time, Josh will come to understand that if he wants to dress himself, he needs to do so according to the family timetable.

The more you find ways to encourage independence, the more time you will save later on.

Principle 5: Delegate Responsibility

Many parents don't give their children chores because they feel that it's easier to "do the chores myself" or they don't want to "burden" their chil-

Great Idea!

Consider the importance of praise and practice. No three-year-old will handle a telephone call perfectly the first couple of times, so expect to practice with her. And praise is absolutely vital to reinforcing the behaviors children are doing well.

dren. Think again. Chores and family responsibility are a gift you give to your children.

When it comes to chores, you'll begin with simple one-step tasks you do with them or you do side by side. If you're cutting vegetables, a toddler can wash or tear lettuce. If you're setting the table, a two-year-old can put the napkins at each place. Preschoolers can learn to put away their toys each evening (with you guiding, helping, or keeping them company), and elementary school children can do dishes or feed and walk the dog. As your child's competence grows, so, too, can the level of chore and responsibility.

One important point: All too often, parents assume that kids absorb knowledge by osmosis, and sometimes they do. But often, training is necessary. Even if your child has watched you set the table many times, show him exactly what you want done the first time. No matter the age of the child or the difficulty of the chore, parents need to follow the same procedure:

- Explain and demonstrate exactly how to do the chore.
- Supervise the performance of the chore.
- Praise your child for mastery.
- Reminders are OK. Some parents find themselves yelling because their child forgot to do a chore. While an older child can be expected to remember, children need to be reminded for a very long time. Don't feel resentful because you need to prompt your child to do something. If it annoys you, set up a reminder system. Your system may involve leaving a note or picture reminder out each day, or establishing a chore chart that your children check daily (but you may have to remind them to look at the chart!).

Young children need parental supervision for most chores, so parents generally choose the tasks on a time-by-time basis. By second or third grade, most children are capable of taking on a regular responsibility, though you may need to remind them now and then.

Working cooperatively as a contributing member of the family improves self-esteem and helps reduce the family stress level (Mom no longer has to fix dinner alone). These are worthy goals for all families.

Teachers say that two of the biggest mistakes parents make are not nipping poor behaviors in the bud and not being consistent in their expectations. "They baby their children or think it [bad behavior] will go away and don't take it seriously. Remember, discipline is a form of love," says one kindergarten teacher.

Limits begin with safety issues like holding your hand when crossing a street and not touching merchandise in a store. They continue on to include establishing bedtimes and other household rules.

No parent wants to serve as a constant rule-enforcer, and the best way to avoid it is to establish schedules and routines. If children are expected to make their bed each morning, they begin to accept such behavior as a matter of routine. In that situation, enforcement usually is unnecessary.

Getting along with siblings provides a challenge in most households. If you're going through a time when there is a lot of bickering or pushing, write down family rules.

Principle 6: Set Limits

Some parents fear setting limits, not wanting to cramp their child's style. But once you've spent time with someone else's child upon whom no limits have been set, you'll see how unattractive an unchecked child is.

Principle 7: Speak to Your Children so They Will Listen

The children are all involved in a game or a television show, and Mom walks by, tossing off the instruction, "Please go wash your hands for supper." Should she be surprised when no one does so?

Parents can choose to speak in ways that will more likely get the desired response. Two ways to make sure your children listen are to work on getting their attention and to speak positively.

Great Idea!

No adult would respond
well to a request to change
ten behaviors, and neither
do children. So focus on
one or two things. Praise
your children often when
things are going well.

Get Their Attention First

Your children may realize you are speaking, but if they don't focus on what you've said, they're not going to respond. The first step in being heard is getting their attention. Here's how:

- Go into the room and speak directly to the child.
- Clap your hands to get the attention of a group of children. Or remember the technique used by teachers: turn the lights on and off.
- Make eye contact, which may mean crouching to be on a child's level.
- Especially with young children, keep your requests simple and your explanations to a minimum. You want them to follow a specific one- or two-step instruction, and the why of it isn't particularly important to most kids.

If you're angry, you may need to physically touch the child by holding both his hands or taking her by the shoulders so that you can see directly into her eyes. Then explain what you're thinking. Speak in your normal voice. Even if you are furious, an angry tone doesn't help.

Find Other Ways to Say No

Children often tune out what they don't want to hear, so the more pleasant your conversations, the better the odds that your kids will pay attention to you. One way you can achieve the behavior you want without having to say no all the time is to find other ways to direct behavior. Try the following ideas:

- Instead of "Quit screaming," say, "Please use your indoor voices."
- Instead of "Stop throwing the ball inside," say, "Let's take the ball outside."

By giving them a positive direction to take, you avoid a head-to-head confrontation over the behavior, and you permit them some feeling of choice in the matter. You're not saying, "Don't play ball," you're just saying, "Don't play ball here."

Use *yes* whenever you can. Instead of saying, "You're too little to go on the merry-go-round," try, "Yes, let's do it together."

A sense of humor also will take you far. "Crawling out of the store is too silly for a four-year-old. What if I crawled out of the store, too? Big kids like you can stand up and hold my hand."

Principle 8: Teach and Show Children How to Express Themselves

Life would be so easy for infants if they could only tell you what's bothering them. The same is true at any age for a child who is unable to make his needs known. The earlier you can teach your children to express their emotions, the better off the family will be.

Model and teach expressing your feelings: "I feel _____ when you _____ because _____." Both you and your children will find that these are powerful words. No one can argue if you restrict your comment to how you feel (who else can know but you?). This way of talking teaches children to come to grips with their feelings.

By serving as your children's emotional tour guide, you can also help them better understand what is happening. If you see another child at the park push your child aside to run up the ladder of the slide first, and your child comes running to you in tears, you can address it head on: "You're upset because that child pushed past you on the slide. Dry your eyes, and I'll go with you to be certain you get to take your turn."

Reflective listening will also help a child puzzle through some hard-to-understand emotions: "It seems what you're telling me is that you feel the kids at school aren't playing fair. Do you think we should talk to the teacher?" While most children have trouble explaining some of the circumstances that crop up, if you reflect back what they seem to be saying, it helps them identify the problem as well.

Principle 9: Anticipate and Redirect

A benefit of being older and wiser than your child is that you can anticipate and prevent certain things. If your child is going through a time where he wants what he wants at the toy store, you'll need to avoid taking him with you to do gift shopping until he's older. Or if he's having trouble adjusting to kindergarten, let him come home and relax afterward. Don't book play dates until he's more settled with the schedule.

Wisdom also permits us to deflect some of our children's bad behavior. If your child has just about had it with trying to put together a puzzle and you feel a tantrum coming on, go to her rescue. Maybe you can help with the puzzle, or maybe it's best to direct her energies elsewhere for a time. Redirection can be a lifesaver in many circumstances.

Principle 10: Teach Problem Solving

"It's Jenny's turn with the scissors, and I know you want to do some cutting, so how can we solve this?" Your four-year-old might come up with anything from asking for the next turn to using the kitchen scissors with your supervision. Praise your children as they think of ways to solve their own problems.

Principle 11: Establish Consequences

The best way to reinforce your dislike of a behavior is to establish consequences. "If you don't get downstairs on time, then I have to dress you," or, "If you don't play nicely with the antique music box, then I have to put it on a high shelf," or, "If you don't remember to put your puzzles away so that your brother doesn't chew on the pieces, I will have to put them away for a week."

Young children don't really understand the meaning of long-term consequences, so establish an immediate cause and effect. With elementary school children, you can begin the process of warning them that a privilege or a right will be removed if they don't take care of the issue that has made you upset.

Some parents have a warning system for consequences: The first time bad behavior is noted, there is a warning. The second time, the parent stresses his unhappiness at the repeated act. The third time, the child loses a privilege.

Principle 12: Be Flexible and Negotiable When Needed

Flexibility in parenting has to do with being wise enough not to make a child do a chore after an upsetting day at school. "You know, I think you might like to just rest right now, so I'm going to feed the cat for you, if you'd like." Your very willingness to understand and to offer to help may actually inspire in him a desire to help someone who loves him enough to want to help out. Or, just as you would welcome it if your spouse said to you, "You had a hard day at work, so put your feet up and I'll fix dinner," your child may, indeed, accept the help.

Negotiation has to do with admitting you don't always know best. Very young children can sometimes make a great case for themselves, and while you needn't always listen, you may want to sometimes. As they become teens, you may find that they will agree to a curfew, but it works best if they have input: "The movie doesn't end until 10:45 P.M., so I'd like to stay out until 11:00 P.M. tonight."

In any negotiation, each side should be able to present a case to the other and get a fair hearing. This builds self-esteem, teaches skills, and demonstrates that you are considerate and appreciative of your child's reasoning skills.

Being good parents involves being smart enough to know when flexibility or negotiation is needed.

Principle 13: Use Reward Systems

Bribing is a mistake, but some types of reward systems can work well. How do you distinguish between a bribe and a reward? A bribe involves a specific promise ("I'll buy you the matchbox car if you don't tell your mother that I backed the car over her geranium bed") for a material reward in a situation where no long-lasting lesson is being learned. The bribe may encourage a child to participate in a deception (as in the example) or it may simply be an effort to get a child to change her behavior this once ("If you don't have a tantrum at the grocery store this time, I'll buy you whatever you want").

A reward system involves a well-thought-out plan. Sometimes the parent wants a new behavior (such as no more hitting) and sometimes child and parent agree that a behavior needs to be changed (such as thumbsucking). In either case, the two of you come up with a plan that good behavior for a given time period (such as no hitting or thumbsucking for a full day) merits some sort of reward (such as a star on a chart). Some children are excited at the thought of earning a star; others may require that a certain number of stars earns them something bigger, such as a trip with Dad to the pancake house for breakfast. One pediatrician says that older children, who are more likely to value money, respond well to financial gain. She tells families to start by giving the child a roll of quarters. The child must give back one quarter for each day that she is unsuccessful at the behavioral change. While you could also agree that your child can earn a quarter for each successful day, the advantage to the "roll of quarters" method is that it is very concrete—the child sees that $10 is within her grasp. A child will certainly value the concept of keeping a full $10 more than she will relish the thought of getting paid a quarter every day.

The best kinds of rewards are the unexpected ones. "I'm so proud of you for how well you've been getting along with your brother, and I think we all should go out to the park and feed the ducks."

Principle 14: Be Consistent

Mean what you say, say what you mean, and stick with it. Children will come to understand that you're serious, and this will save you much time over the years. Consider consistency to be a foundation on which a child can build. If you establish certain rules and behaviors that are followed in your family, you've provided your children with a starting point from which to make decisions for themselves. If they witness that Mom and Dad are always ready for work on time—and see that they are praised for being ready on time themselves—then the children know when the teacher wants the class to be ready to go out to recess, the proper thing to do is to put away schoolwork and get ready for recess. As time goes on and they see that when Mom and Dad consider a decision and say no, there is no point in whining or sassing back about the decision: no means

Trouble Zone!

Times of transition are hard for most of us. Adults don't like having to put down the novel they're reading to make dinner, nor do they want to stop a phone conversation they're enjoying. Children take major issue with transitions: "Why do I have to leave the playground now?" "Do we really have to stop the game to go to Grandma's?" Who can blame them? It *is* hard to stop doing something fun for something that might not be as enjoyable.

Many parents have good luck with a countdown warning system. Here's how it works:

1. "Kevin, we're leaving for the store in ten minutes, so I need you to finish what you are doing."
2. "Kevin, we're leaving in five minutes, so please go to the bathroom."
3. "Kevin we're going in one minute. Please come down and put on your coat."

You can vary the warning times, but when you first introduce this method, you'll need to walk your child through it. With the first finish-what-you're-doing warning, you need to go to your child to make certain he heard you. Get an acknowledgment. At the five-minute warning, walk with him to the bathroom. Then walk with him to the coat closet as you give the one-minute warning.

When children are playing, swimming, or having a great time, your warning system is still vital to your success in achieving cooperation. In the beginning, you may have to physically retrieve children from the game or the pool so they know that you mean what you say. The ten-year-old with whom you have used this method since toddlerhood will cooperate quickly, as she won't want you to come to the side of the pool to get her in front of her friends when you give her the final "It's time to go." If you're just beginning the system with your family, be persistent. Over time your children will understand what behavior is expected of them.

Bigger transitions, such as going on a trip or starting school or day camp, require additional preparation. Check with a librarian for books on anything from a first plane trip to the first day of nursery school. Also discuss in advance some of the fun activities or occurrences that will happen on the trip or in school.

Begin these discussions well in advance of the event. That way, if your child is particularly anxious, you can actually discuss it less and less as the time draws nearer. On the day of the Big Event, your child will draw on the banked information you provided with books and discussions, and that will help a child make an easier transition.

By nature, some people adapt more readily to any type of change than other people do. Even so, establishing a warning system and showing how to prepare can help a child of any temperament adjust more easily.

no. The open-minded parent will listen to a well-reasoned presentation from a child who still wants to present more information for the parental decision process. (Also refer to Chapter 5.)

If your child stays with a caregiver, be certain he or she is up to speed on how you and your spouse want certain behavioral issues handled. If Grandma comes occasionally and "spoils" your child, don't worry about it. Your child will be able to know when best behavior is expected.

What About Spanking?

"I was spanked, so I don't see anything wrong with it."

"I'm going to spank them for their own good."

"I don't really spank. I just give a quick swat."

These are the comments you often hear from parents about spanking, but unfortunately, this is a behavioral technique that simply doesn't work. While spanking relieves a parent's frustration and may stop misbehavior briefly, researchers for the American Academy of Pediatrics have found that spanking is the least effective discipline method. It makes children feel ashamed, resentful, and helpless, and it doesn't teach them how to resolve conflict. What should the toddler do instead of shoving when he wants to get in line? How should a third-grader handle her feelings instead of talking back when she is really upset? Studies show that spanking correlates with higher levels of aggression in children; it demonstrates physical violence—something you certainly don't want your child to emulate—without teaching an alternative approach.

Proper Use of Time-Outs

Time-outs are a highly misunderstood behavior technique, so it is important to understand why this chapter did not introduce time-outs as a technique for improving behavior.

People often say, "Time-outs don't work." Time-outs often fail because they are used improperly. Parents sometimes assume time-outs are a form of punishment: "I'm putting you in time-out, so go to your room!" Well, of course, this isn't going to work. First of all, it may be difficult to march an upset child to his room. Once the child is there, if he is having a tantrum, it may not be safe to leave him. If he's calm enough, where is the lesson? Children probably think, "So I get sent to my room, and I can play with my Legos, and no one is going to bother me."

Time-outs are exactly what the word means—a cooling-off period for times when behavior is out of control or tempers are flaring. (If you are the one who is angry, you may want to give yourself a time-out.) Here's how to achieve that purpose:

- Use time-outs to create calm so that the upsetting issue can be dealt with.
- You may have to hold or sit with the child throughout the time-out. That's acceptable. If the child is really upset, you won't be able to communicate what behavior upset you until he feels in control again.
- The place where you have a child sit should be within your vision. This isn't about banishing the kid; it's about removing her from the environment where things were getting out of hand.
- Time-outs should be no longer in minutes than the child's age in years. Your three-year-old can be in time-out for three minutes. It is unrealistic to think a time-out can last longer.
- If you are upset, make certain the children are safe, and put yourself in time-out for a few minutes. (Sorry, but unless another adult is at home, you can't stay for as long as your age!)
- Once you and your child are calm, talk about the upsetting situation and discuss finding a solution. For example, if one afternoon two siblings haven't been able to share, what are some ways to solve this problem?

Time-outs help you teach a skill that will last a lifetime. (No one in the workplace is ever sent away with the instructions, "Now go to your office and just think about what you've done!") Time-outs teach these lessons:

Trouble Zone!

Avoid trouble with these parenting don'ts:

- Don't bribe.
- If you want to be heard, don't criticize too much or yell or nag.
- Avoid ending your instructions with "OK?"
- Don't run a democracy.
- Don't give in to whining.
- Don't save your kids by doing things for them.
- Don't nag about every little thing; choose your battles.
- Don't embarrass.
- Don't threaten: "You'll talk when I'm done."
- Don't send them to their room.

- Don't vent your anger on other people.
- Remove yourself, if necessary, and calm down.
- Return to the situation and discuss with others possible ways to solve the problem.

As you read the remainder of this book, you'll find that the fourteen principles outlined in this chapter are used again and again. They work.

PART TWO

Stopping Bad Behavior

CHAPTER 3

Tantrums

More than some other bad behaviors, tantrums push all the parental buttons. Unspoken parental reactions generally involve a flushed face, an increased heart rate, sweaty palms, and intense feelings of irritation. Maybe tantrums are so vexing because so often they occur in public, when you're tired, and when you've worked hard to do something pleasant with your child.

The Oh-So-Embarrassing Tantrum

It's Thanksgiving. Your parents have finally agreed to include your in-laws in the family celebration, which also involves extended-family members who get together just once a year. It's been fun seeing everyone, but it's been stressful as well. Being certain the in-laws feel comfortable and making small talk with the cousins you see only once a year has been exhausting. Finally, it's time to leave. You go to get your six-year-old and your "almost-four-year-old" from the den, where the kids have been playing. The three-year-old, who has been happily playing on the floor with a cousin, flops down on her back, crying loudly, "You're so mean! I hate you and Daddy! I'm not leaving! I want to stay at Grandma's, because she loves me more than you do!"

Conversations in the living room (not to mention those in the den) quiet down because of your daughter's shrieking. No amount of begging quiets her, and you wish you could sink into the floor. You and your

Tantrums don't only happen during the terrible twos. Kids have emotional outbursts from the time they become mobile until they start school (and sometimes beyond). Understanding why and how children erupt this way can help us empathize, cope, and even cut down on the behavior.

spouse are both tired from the day. How are you ever going to get out of the house?

The "Couldn't You Scream a Little Quieter?" Tantrum

Who doesn't have a child who has had a tantrum at the grocery store or a toy store? At the grocery it's likely to be over a coveted box of sugar-coated cereal or a kind of cookie you unsually don't buy. At the toy store, the kicking and screaming start with a desire for the latest toy advertised on television and escalates when your little darling realizes you're going to buy a present for her cousin's birthday and nothing at all for her.

The "I Can't Believe This Is Happening" Tantrum

You've just spent a full afternoon at the playground. You've been the model parent. You've pushed him on the swings, you've followed him on the monkey bars, you've sat by the sandbox to supervise play. It's finally time to go home and fix dinner, but your attempt to put him in the stroller (or car seat) is met by full resistance. Arching his back and refusing to sit, he screams and screams and screams. Most parents can't help but think, "So this is the thanks I get for your nice afternoon. Next time we'll just stay home."

Unfortunately for parents, tantrums are a normal stage in development, starting during the famed terrible twos and sometimes continuing for a few years after that. Here's what you need to do to speed through this period in your child's development.

Understanding the Cause

"Forget the cause! Just tell me what to do when he's screaming!" you may be thinking, and you're absolutely right. Once you're in the midst of a tantrum, you don't really *care* what is causing it; you just want it to stop! All the same, it is helpful to know why tantrums happen because this can partially lead you to ways to prevent them. (If your child is screaming and trying to tear this book out of your hands, skip ahead to the information on how to handle the tantrum. You can read this background information later.) The following causes cover most situations:

- *Frustration in their pursuit of autonomy*—Toddlers have many tasks ahead of them, but a primary one is achieving autonomy from you. They've realized they are separate beings and are aware of the growing benefits (being able to play with siblings, being able to do things for themselves and not be dependent, being able to follow their own interests at the playground). The only problem is that it's really hard for them to button a shirt, and tying a shoe is impossible. Carrying a dish from the table to the sink is doable—most of the time. Petting the dog *gently* is a task worth mastering. Almost every moment of the day is spent attempting new challenges or perfecting the old ones, and it gets downright frustrating. Tantrums arise from pent-up frustration or when children are interrupted in a task that, it seems to them, is taking "forever."
- *Anger over being denied what they want*—As children become their own person, they also develop opinions. They are very self-centered, so fairness means nothing to them. If you could hear their little brains clack through some daily issues that arise, you would hear something like this as a tantrum begins to erupt:

  "Leave playgroup? Why should we? I don't care if you need to go to the grocery store."
  "What's unhealthy about cookies? The man on TV gives them to his kids."
  "Put away the blocks? I'm happy with them right here."
  "If you're buying my friend Billy this toy for his birthday, then you ought to buy me one, too."

  For children to be able to handle situations like these maturely, they need to develop a greater understanding of the world around them. You won't see this level of understanding in a two-year-old, and

Did You Know?

Most tantrums are about feelings, not misbehavior. A tantrum is emotional overload. It's a buildup of unexpressed emotion, which becomes unbearable for the child—the psychological equivalent of severe physical pain. With a tantrum, you need to look for the tantrum pattern or the reason it came.

a tired five-year old (or older!) may revert to bad behavior over these issues as well.

- *Fatigue and hunger*—Our bodies are the great levelers. No matter how grown-up children act sometimes, fatigue and hunger can make them regress and display all their most dislikable qualities.
- *Desire for attention*—Sometimes tantrums arise because a child is feeling confused or neglected, and negative attention is better than no attention at all.

Of course, at the root of all tantrums is anger. Therefore, an important part of helping children avoid tantrums is providing them with outlets for their anger. Doing that begins with managing your own anger well.

Be a Good Role Model

As always, parents must set a good example. If your child is easily angered, consider how you handle your own anger and negative feelings:

- Don't lose control yourself. When your child is out of control, it is more important than ever that you remain in control. Believe it or not, children don't like flying into a rage. Weakness or a responsive rage from you will just alarm your child more.
- Don't ever take your child's tantrums personally. Even if a tantrum erupts over a rule you're enforcing, the tantrum really isn't about you.
- Consider when and why you get mad. That innocent two-year-old may not have a very large vocabulary, but he understands very well what the emotions are if Dad is steamed because the light is red or the other driver "is an idiot." If you demonstrate this type of anger in situations over which you have no control, you're likely to see this type of anger in your child.

Parents who are so stressed that their anger pops up randomly would do well to investigate ways to relax. And it's never too late to start expressing your feelings with the "I feel _____ when you _____ because _____" method (see Chapter 2).

What to Do: The Basics About Tantrums

Whether you're at home, school, or a store, the basic steps in managing a tantrum are the same:

- *Remain calm and don't lose your temper*—No matter how angry you are at what is happening, lashing back at your child conveys the wrong message. Your child won't listen anyway.
- *Don't try to reason with your child*—A child having a tantrum is not one to be reasoned with. The breath you expend will be wasted, and he will have won Round 1—he got your attention.
- *Don't give in to his request*—We've all thought, "Oh, heck, I'll just buy her the stupid cereal so we can get out of here." But the moment you do, you immediately become a hostage to buying what your little dictator wants every time you go to the store.
- *Don't bribe*—Tantrums must not achieve their goals.
- *If you're in public, ignore public opinion*—Despite the "what a terrible parent" glares you are getting from some, many parents understand what you're going through.
- *Find a safe, quiet place for your child*—If you're at home, ignore the tantrum. If you are concerned for a young child's safety, carry her to a safe place (crib? playpen?) to finish the tantrum. "I'll be back when you calm down," should be your message. Try going to her and giving her a hug or a pat: "I love you, but your screaming hurts my ears. When you calm down, I'll come back."
- *Leave the public place if necessary*—If your child does not calm down within a minute or two, try to leave the store or museum or church—wherever you are—if you can. If you've got a cartload of groceries, you might try asking a clerk if you can park it near her for a moment so that you can help your child calm down. Store clerks will generally hold potential purchases at the counter until you can come back.

At Wit's End

"When your mother is mad and asks you, 'Do I look stupid?' it's best not to answer her."

—Meghan, age thirteen

"You should never laugh at your dad if he's mad or screaming at you."

—Jason, age twelve

"Every time I am at home and I am getting on my parents' nerves, they wish I were at camp. And every time I'm at camp and nothing's bothering them, they miss me."

—Ashley, age twelve

- *Hold your child if he's physically out of control*—He doesn't like feeling this way either. Within a few minutes, most kids will be calmed by being held.

When your child calms down, describe what you're calling a tantrum, and offer alternatives. "When you lie on the floor and kick and scream, I'm just not going to do what you want. I can't understand what you're saying when you're screaming, so you need to calm down so we can talk about things." Once the child is calm, don't accede to her wishes, but you can say, "Next time you want something, please ask calmly. Then maybe we'll be able to discuss it." While the desired outcome (from the child's point of view) may not be possible even with calm discussion, a quiet back and forth will permit you to hammer out a solution: "I can't buy you a toy today because we're only shopping for Jamie's present. However, when we get home, we're going to start a birthday list, and we'll put this on the top of the list of what you want for your birthday." This kind of response acknowledges his very serious desire for a particular toy, and while you haven't agreed to buy the toy, you have agreed to take his request seriously. That's an important life lesson.

Offer ways for your child to vent her anger. You might say, "We all feel angry sometimes because we can't do what we want. Here are some ways to get rid of those feelings without upsetting everyone around you." (You can suggest some of the ideas described later under "Anger Management.") Tantrums would seem like a perfect occasion for a time-out, but unfortunately, young children (under age six) throwing a tantrum are out of control to the point of not being able to listen, and you're wasting your time and breath trying to make them do something they are incapable of doing anyway.

Distract as soon as possible. You might say, "I'm glad you're calming down. Let's go for a walk," or, "You're quieting down so nicely. Will you come sit with me—or help me in the kitchen?" Children really do want to be saved from the violence of their own emotions. Give your child a hug and reassure her that you still love her.

Even school-age children (six and older) can become so distressed that they'll be out of control in a tantrum-like way. Acknowledge that they are upset, and ask them to go to their room until they calm down. By this age, most children understand that their behavior is socially unacceptable and that poor behavior has consequences—in this case, removal from other people. Once the child is calm, the two of you can find a solution. The child is not being punished, but you are teaching him or her a life strategy: When you get really upset about something, it's best to remove yourself until you can quiet down. That way you don't say or do anything you might regret.

Finally, reinforce good behavior. If you've had a successful trip to the mall or a visit somewhere where tantrums tend to erupt, be sure to praise your child for behaving so well!

Anger Management

At the root of a child's tantrum are negative feelings that need to be released. (No normal child misbehaves when a favorite uncle takes him to a baseball game or an ice-cream parlor.) Being human brings with it all types of feelings, both positive and negative. While we can't stop negative feelings (yes, he really does have to stop playing and take a bath; yes, she really must let you focus on the grocery shopping), we need to teach children what to do when they feel angry.

Sometimes it is enough to distract or divert the child from the anger-producing situation. Toddlers and preschoolers can often be pointed in a new direction. "You can't go with your brother to the playground because he's riding his bike, but let's go see if Sally and her mom will walk to the playground with us."

Help your children learn to identify angry feelings. Not even adults always recognize that the uncomfortable feeling they have is anger. If you can help your children identify when they feel angry, you have already put them on the road to feeling better. When your two-year-old has his bucket taken away by a playmate in the sandbox, he feels angry (and may cry or bean the other kid). The four-year-old who is having a wonderful time playing with her friend is going to be angry when you say it's time to go home (and will probably sulk or not cooperate). The eight-year-old who gets a bad cold right before the first scout sleepover will be furious

Great Idea!

You can empathize with how upset your child is, but don't try to reason with her. Say, "I'll talk to you when you quiet down."

when told he's too sick to go (and may talk back to you or even throw something in frustration at being left out). Helping your son or daughter label these feelings ("You feel angry because . . .") is a first step toward wrestling with those unpleasant feelings we all know so well.

Acknowledge your child's feelings. Often, kids have tantrums over things that we, too, would have tantrums over if we weren't grown-ups. Well, maybe you wouldn't have a tantrum over a Snickers bar, but what about a KitKat? And if given the choice between leaving your friend's home or staying there to continue to play—these are no-brainers! To coexist with other people in the world, none of us can do exactly what we want to do. Who would fix meals, make the beds, pick up garbage, or get work done? Unfortunately, we have to shoulder responsibilities. That said, you'll bring the tantrum stage of childhood to a quicker end if you're sympathetic (when relevant) but firm. "I know you don't want to put away your game, but we have to leave to go pick up your sister now."

Suggest a way to release anger. Whether you suggest running around to get some exercise or simply saying, "I am *so* mad!" help your child deal with the pent-up energy that generally goes along with feeling upset. Note your own methods of release. Some people scrub, others jog, others treat themselves to a quiet bath or go off on their own for a time—all as a way to get a grip when emotions feel out of control. You and your child could make a list of ways to expend negative energy. The first several of these suggestions are most appropriate for a younger child; older, school-age children need to find ways to get rid of angry feelings without drawing attention to themselves, as with the last few suggestions.

- Make angry noises—suggest thinking of lots of different ones.
- Count as far as you can in a grumpy voice.
- Make up an angry dance.
- Walk around the room with great big steps.
- Get out clay or play dough and squeeze it hard.
- Think about what else you could do or have, since you can't have what you want.
- Wrap your arms around yourself really tightly so you don't feel so angry anymore.
- Take deep yoga breaths. While this is good for older children, you can use it with younger ones, too. Even if your child doesn't know

what yoga is, the word is tailor-made to interest little tongues. Using your own funny voice, you might suggest, "Let's take deep yo-ga breaths." If you're lucky, the very start of you taking a deep yo-ga breath can come to remind your child not to start a tantrum.

Avoiding Tantrums

In most cases, kids are fairly predictable. They have tantrums when they are tired or hungry (or both) or when certain situations put them under a lot of stress. The kindest thing you can do for the family is try to anticipate what brings on a tantrum and then try to avoid it. Here are some suggestions:

- Avoid the obvious triggers. If your child is incapable of going to a toy store right now without having a tantrum, do your shopping for birthday presents without him.
- If restaurants send your toddler over the top, take a break from eating out. Take-out meals can offer parents a change without putting kids through the stress of going to a restaurant when they are already tired from a long day. To ease back into the routine of going out for a meal, try a pancake house for breakfast or lunch—at a time when your child is more likely to be better behaved.
- If your child is having trouble sharing a particular toy or group of toys when friends come over and being forced to share has set off tantrums, put the items away. Say, "You don't seem to like to share your Bear Family, and I can understand how you feel, since they mean a lot to you. Let's put them on a high shelf in the closet and get them out when your friend goes home. (Pause.) This means that the other toys in your room are all to be shared. When you go to Michelle's house, she shares with you."
- Use humor when you can. If you sense a tantrum in the making, start a game:

TODDLER: I want cotton candy!
PARENT: Well, I want a pretty ring.
TODDLER: Give me candy!

Trouble Zone!

Consult your pediatrician if:

- tantrums last more than ten minutes
- your child is older than two and a half and having major tantrums every day
- your child is younger than two and a half and having three or four major tantrums per day

PARENT: *(in a light tone, handing her imaginary candy)* Here's some candy, yum, yum. Now please give me a ring—I'll let you wear it.

If all has gone well in this diversion, your toddler will hand you an imaginary ring, and you can pretend to put it on and admire it. As your child becomes more familiar with this tactic, your game may have to become more complex, but again, working at diversion is better than a full-blown tantrum.

- No matter what the family's destination, describe beforehand the behavior that you expect. "We're going into the mall, and I need you to stay in your stroller while Mommy goes to two stores. After that, we'll have a snack, and you can go on the restaurant's merry-go-round." Or: "We're going to visit Aunt Betty's house because she hurt her leg. She has lots of breakable china, so I'm bringing toys for you to play with. We'll only stay for twenty minutes, and I need you to sit by me and play with your things." (If your child is getting restless after fifteen minutes, too bad for Aunt Betty—you'll visit her again another day.)
- Transitions often set off tantrums. Refer to Chapter 3 for ideas about handling transitions.
- Offer choices. Since frustration at not being able to be independent is at the root of many of your child's tantrums, offer choices whenever you can. The child who is offered a choice of sandwich or soup will not have a tantrum. The child who is simply given soup may well be annoyed at not having a chance for an opinion.
- Enlist your child's help. "We need ten items at the grocery, and one of the things we need is crackers. We're going to count the first nine things I have to get, and then you get to pick the kind of cracker."

Head Banging

Approximately 20 percent of all toddlers bang their heads on purpose, and boys are three times more likely to do it than girls. This behavior sometimes arises out of frustration or for attention, and parents think of it as a type of tantrum. However, head banging also is done for other reasons, such as pain relief or comfort, particularly if a child is having ear pain. When accompanied by a rocking motion, children use head banging as a method of self-comfort.

Don't become alarmed by head banging or make a big deal out of it. You do want to make certain your child won't hurt himself, so check where he bangs to be certain there is nothing sharp. If your child rocks in his crib as part of the activity, examine the bolts of the bed periodically to be certain that nothing is loosening.

In most cases, head banging ends by about age four. If your child continues or you are concerned, check with your doctor.

The behavior may be perfectly normal (for example, in a situation where your family has moved or there has been some other recent upheaval in your child's life). In that case, you'll get some reassurance and some advice based on what the doctor knows about your particular child.

Usually tantrums are not a cause for concern, and the stage generally slows down and diminishes on its own. As children become more capable, their frustration will drop. This, too, will mean fewer tantrums as children gain control over their lives.

Clinging and Shyness

At preschool drop-off, they are a common sight for the first few weeks of school—the clingers. These toddlers and early preschoolers have trouble letting go. For those of us who have parented a shy or clingy child, we know the pain of raising a clinger. While there's something a little endearing about the fact that they just love being with us, we can't help but envy parents whose kids blithely skip into the classroom, eager to start work in the block corner.

Compared to clinging, shyness seems mild, harmless, hardly a bad behavior, but consider this situation: The family is at a friend's house for a picnic. Four-year-old Margaret sits happily in her mother's lap. Margaret's older sister plays with the other children, many of whom are new to her. The other kids ignore Margaret's behavior, but when a friendly mother comes over to suggest that Margaret go join her own four-year-old in the games going on in the backyard, Margaret shyly hides her face in her mother's shoulder and listens while her mother says, "Margaret is shy. She'll stay with me for a while."

Unfortunately for Margaret, by the time she feels comfortable with leaving her mother, raindrops have started to fall, and the picnic comes to a hasty end. Margaret's sister leaves the group with promises of meeting up another time to continue the game; Margaret takes her mother's hand, and they get in the car. Margaret stands at risk of always being on the sidelines.

While no parent would argue about clinginess being a bad behavior, shyness is rarely thought of in this way because for so long people have

Did You Know?

Some children are shy by nature. They are more likely than other children to be slow to warm up in new social situations. Research is showing evidence that shyness can partly be hereditary. In fact, heredity may play a larger part in shyness than in any other personality trait.

Some experts say that when it comes to shyness, the way to tell the difference between nature and nurture is to consider the age at which shyness exhibits itself. If your child exhibits shyness—fear of strangers and new situations, avoidance of eye contact—from infancy, then she probably inherited it. If it begins later, then there may be environmental factors. Did you move recently? Is there a new baby? Do you have reason to think your child is being teased at school?

---

felt, upon hearing that someone is shy, "Well, that's just how it is." And while the child who is shy and retiring causes no real harm, no disruption, and no angst to those around her, she is doing a terrible disservice to herself. As you saw in the opening story, Margaret's sister took advantage of the two hours they were at the picnic. She met new kids, she interacted with them, and they created new games. Whether or not Margaret's sister Marian ever sees these kids again, she has practiced some life skills that will help her later on. Margaret, on the other hand, stayed with her mother and observed the other kids until staying with her mother just got too deadly boring. Margaret's delayed entry into the games makes her a bit player, more likely to be victimized than viewed as a leader. In the game of life, this is a loss for Margaret.

While the Margarets of the world may always be more withdrawn than the Marians, parents who tolerate, and thereby support, the shyness are missing an opportunity to help their child. By encouraging shy children to overcome some of the anxiety they feel when encountering new people and new situations, parents can make a real difference. It's as important to work at socializing a shy child as it is to teach an aggressive child to stop to think of others.

Here's what you can do to help your clingy child and your shy child become more comfortable in their surroundings. We'll also talk about the "Only Mommy do it!" clinger, as that issue, too, is better off addressed early.

Understanding the Cause

Clinging is a normal phase that most toddlers go through, though some pass through it more quickly than others. It stems from the work of becoming their own person. Sometimes the process of separating from you is just too scary, and clinging helps them give up you, their "security blanket," a little bit at a time. Parents who work outside the home often worry that this contributes to clinginess, but it's really the child's personality that makes the difference. Even so, if you've taken your child to school and aren't usually the one to do so, there may be additional clinging because it's a special occasion.

Shyness may be an adaptive mechanism used to help people cope with new situations and extra stimuli. Shy people do not really want to run away and hide; they are feeling a mixture of emotions—fear and interest as well as tension and pleasure. That's why observing a situation for a time helps them warm up.

Shyness can be a normal response to an overwhelming social experience. By withdrawing temporarily, children can gain a sense of control. As they observe and then gain some experience with the social situation that is frightening them, their shyness wanes.

Stress can cause any child to feel hesitant and therefore shy. If other children taunt or tease, or if the child has an awkward entry into the situation, these circumstances reinforce the shyness.

Some aspects of shyness are learned, and by labeling a child "shy" or cajoling a reticent child to enter a social situation, parents unfortunately reinforce shy behavior.

Be a Good Role Model

If you are a friendly person who enjoys other people, you will doubtless model openness and willingness to meet new people—a healthy trait for your child to observe. If new encounters are a little more difficult for you,

Great Idea!

When you are in social situations together, model introducing yourself to new people. (Always do so with a big smile on your face; see "The Power of the Smile," later in this chapter.) Let your child see that you're not afraid to step forward and meet the new head of the nursery school or greet a mother who has just moved into the neighborhood. You can even talk about how it's really nice to introduce yourself to new people because it makes them feel more at ease.

opening up to others isn't such a bad type of behavior to start practicing. And even if new situations are difficult for you, you needn't discuss that with your child. Our children frequently become braver than we are, more outgoing than we are, and become kids we are really quite proud of because they exceed what we are. Don't burden them with predictions like, "You're just shy because I am."

What to Do: The Basics About Clinging and Shyness

Here is an approach that usually helps children overcome their clinging and shyness:

- Don't label. Whether a toddler is clinging or the preschooler is "being shy," parents frequently look for a way to excuse what they view as embarrassing behavior by saying, "Oh, she's just shy." The very act of labeling a child increases the odds that the stage will continue for longer than necessary. In addition, your child could grow up labeling herself as shy, and this can affect who she is for the rest of her life: "I can't try out for the high school play. I'm shy," or, "I could never speak in front of a big audience at work. I'm shy." Don't saddle your child with a burden like that when she's just a child.
- If possible, expose your child to a new environment ahead of time. If your child is starting at a new day-care center or going somewhere new for a play date without you, try to visit the new place in advance.
- Acknowledge your child's feelings. Feeling ill at ease about trying something new or entering a group can be painful—why not stick with Dad? Tell your child you understand how he feels and that you'll stay with him for a few minutes, but then he needs to venture out with the rest of the kids.
- After a brief adjustment period, release your child gently into the social fray. If you're leaving your child at nursery school, you'll have a good deal of guidance and help from the teachers. Don't undo the progress your child will undoubtedly make at school by staying on play dates or in other situations that are age-appropriate expectations for your child. (See "Helping a Young Child Achieve Social Confidence.")

Trouble Zone!

For the most part, clinging and shyness are nothing to worry about. They are normal behaviors that you and your child can work through. However, you might want to consult an expert in two situations:

1. If an outgoing child suddenly starts acting shy and withdrawn with the behavior continuing for a time, check with the pediatrician for advice. Something may be bothering your child.

2. Sometimes children are shy in only one particular environment. Have you ever heard someone comment, "Oh, he never speaks in school." This may simply reflect that child's opinion of the teacher or the classroom environment, but it may signal something more serious. (See Chapter 12 for information on this problem, called *selective mutism*.)

- Establish a good-bye routine that lets your child know it's time for you to go. Teachers recommend a pattern of a certain number of kisses or family sayings like, "See you later, Alligator"—anything that you and your child agree is your last activity together before you have to leave.

Helping a Young Child Achieve Social Confidence

Note: This section addresses ideas for children age six and younger. For suggestions for an older child, refer to the next section.

When it comes to social competence and building confidence, experience is the best teacher. If your child is shy, the best way to build confidence is to create safe environments where she can interact.

One of the first places for this is nursery school. Trust the nursery school teachers. No parent has ever had to stay by a child's side all the way through high school—children can and will separate. Teachers will eventually get each child involved.

At school and elsewhere, suggest ways for your child to become busy so that he quits thinking of you. Whether you're permitted to walk her to the art table or have to stay at the door will depend on the school, but if a child can get involved with an activity, separation becomes easier.

If you're concerned about how your child is doing in nursery school, ask for a conference. Don't discuss your concerns at drop-off or pickup. It's unfair to the teachers and the other kids, and there's a very good chance your child will overhear what is said. Some schools have one-way windows (mirror on the classroom side, window on the inlooking side), and they might suggest you stop by midmorning to observe (unseen) for yourself.

When you're with your child at family or neighborhood gatherings or at your parents' group, pay attention to how your child is doing. Praise her when she reaches out to join others. "It was terrific the way you went off to play with your cousins today. Did you have fun?" If your child isn't making much progress, you can praise other children who are outgoing and show her the example of another way to interact. If a classmate of your child's approaches you at nursery school drop-off and asks for help with the stuck zipper on his backpack, you might say to your child, "I'm so glad Brian came over to us. The teachers were busy, so I'm pleased that he felt he could ask someone else for help."

With a shy toddler, you may not want to enroll him in a wild toddler gym class just yet. Look into an interactive music class where the pace might be a little slower and he will have the opportunity to do a lot of observing before he needs to interact.

"Can I play?" is a risky question for a child to ask. There is always the strong risk of being turned down. Other strategies for joining in will avoid those dangerous words. Help your child learn these strategies:

- Suggest simply joining in. If a few children are playing in the block corner, suggest that your child simply start playing beside them. In most cases, the newcomer will simply be absorbed into the game. Learning to include oneself is a very helpful strategy in the teen years, when ostracizing members of a class or a group becomes a prime activity.
- Teach your child to ask, "What are you playing?" Rehearse with your child some ways to involve herself once the basic game has been explained. If the other children say, "We're playing house," she might reply, "How about if I'm one of the sisters?" (The role of Mom is likely

taken.) If the others turn down your child's proposal without offering a new role, then she might suggest being a friendly neighbor who drops by. Your child will need some practice with this strategy, but it's a great way to stretch the imagination and get included at the same time.

Set up play dates with carefully selected children. First ask your child with whom he wants to play. If he offers no suggestions, check with the nursery school teacher. Look for calm children and parents or nannies who will be sensitive to your child's needs. The first play date should be at your house; the second one should be at the other child's. (Don't pamper your child by letting all dates be at home.) If you explain to the host parent that you'll stay for a few minutes to get your child settled, she will likely be willing to check a little more frequently to make certain your child is comfortable.

If the play date is only thirty minutes but you are able to leave, you have achieved success. Praise your child for how well he did. Chances are good that the next play date will be longer.

As you meet success with one or two children, expand your social outreach. Later on, your child may be ready for that wild and woolly gym class!

Help your child think of fun things to do on play dates, both at home and away. "I really love it when Jimmy comes over, because the two of you have so much fun on the swing set," or, "It will be fun to visit Alex's house now that they have the new puppy. I think I'll come in with you for a minute to see it."

Some children have difficulty talking with adults, and you—and teachers—can help with this. Most adults welcome being approached by children, so if you let your child practice conversation with your friends or other significant adults, this shyness will likely go away soon.

New baby-sitters offer a special challenge. To ease the transition, build in overlap so that the sitter is there for a few minutes before you have to leave. Remember what every parent tells you: Your child will adapt to the situation as soon as you are out of ear range. If you have regular child care during the day but use different people at night, consider putting together an "I'm going out" kit filled with special toys that are for the exclusive use of a new sitter and your child. When you get home, gather the toys and put the bag away for the next time you go out.

Did You Know?

According to research, more than 50 percent of people think of themselves as shy.

Helping an Older Child Achieve Social Confidence

School-age children can also have difficulty feeling comfortable in a social group, and there are ways you can go about helping them. As with younger children, pay attention to their friendships—do they have friends where the relationships are reciprocal? If not, you can encourage inviting some different children from school to your home for play dates or to go to a movie with your family. Maybe something will develop. Also encourage your child to seek out kids he knows from Sunday school or from an after-school activity. Lots of children find their best friendships away from the classroom, and while you'd like to have them have good friends at school, the important thing is that they have friends whom they really enjoy, regardless of whether or not they are schoolmates.

Neglecting to include themselves is often a major issue with children of all ages who feel outside a group. Whether your child is three or nine (or even fifteen), talk to her about finding ways to simply join into activities. Boys of all ages are generally willing to accept almost anyone in a game of pickup basketball or touch football. If your son isn't athletic, remind him to seek out the kids who have similar hobbies and interests; they will likely be happy to accept him. While girls as young as elementary school sometimes purposely exclude a child, many times the exclusion occurs because the girl doesn't know how to take the social leap and join in. Talk to your daughter about where she encounters difficulties and strategize ways that she can make herself part of the group. If the exclusion is occurring at school, the teacher may offer helpful advice as to how your daughter can blend in and be included.

The Power of the Smile

No matter the age of the person, it is hard for others to resist someone who joins them while wearing a smile. Encourage your child in his smiling ability: "Billy, you have a great smile! I feel so good when I see it." While the shy child may not smile when first entering a new situation, a smile will come more easily if the family has reinforced it.

Smiling communicates friendliness and the fact that you will welcome someone speaking to you. This is a good message for a shy child to communicate, as he or she generally does eventually want to be acknowledged and included.

The child without a smile may look scared or frightened. Such a face encourages more powerful children to become aggressive.

Conversational Skills

The school-age child is ready to learn good conversational skills, and those who excel at this are destined to go far in life. Here are some ways to develop those skills in your child:

- Teach your child to ask people questions about themselves. Demonstrate this skill and talk to your child about possible questions to ask: "What's your favorite TV show?" "Do you have a pet?" "What games do you like to play?" Children who learn to do this not only gather fascinating information from both adults and kids, but they eventually develop a concern for others as a result. Instead of being turned inward all the time, they begin to observe what it's like to be a child whose mother is regularly late to pick him up or how it feels to be cut out of the group. Empathy will follow.
- Help your child practice answering questions. If someone says, "What's your favorite animal?" can your child come back with a ready answer? (It's also OK to think about an answer, so tell her that, too.) If you have nearby grandparents, they are wonderfully well suited for helping your child practice answering questions.
- Teach your child to give and accept compliments. Again, this is a lovely way to break the ice in a challenging situation. "I really like your sandals," and, "You're really good at basketball," are both comments that get a relationship off to a strong start. Also teach your child the art of the simple "thank you!" when someone compliments him on something.
- Teach appropriateness. While conversational skills are a lifelong gift to the children who learn them, parents also need to teach when and with whom it is appropriate to start conversations. When the bell rings and all the rest of the class is getting into their seats, you do not want your son in the front of the room asking the teacher if she thinks it's

At Wit's End

"Where parents do too much for their children, the children will not do much for themselves."
—Elbert Hubbard, nineteenth-century American author

a good idea for him to ask for a puppy for Christmas. Children also need to be coached and reminded about stranger danger. They should not strike up conversations with adults (or teens) they don't know, and they should report to an adult they know if they are approached by a stranger. Children need to be on alert for the fact that a stranger who needs help "looking for my puppy" or any similar request is a person to avoid. If the stranger's need is legitimate, that person should talk to the parent or the teacher (or whoever the supervising adult is) before he or she approaches a child with such a request.

A Word About Birthday Parties

I expect experts would say that even a shy or clingy child should be able to stay at a birthday party. But I'm a mom, and I'm going to offer my own advice here.

Birthday parties can be wild! The parent running the party may or may not be experienced or comfortable with large groups of kids, and the adult-to-child ratio is often less than ideal. Drop me down with forty-five kids at a local play-gym free-for-all, and I, too, would like a friendly hand to hold!

As a mom, I stayed at many parties, primarily with my middle daughter. Even at a small at-home party, the birthday kid tends to lose it, and the parents are often frantic about just getting the party over with — not an atmosphere conducive to making a somewhat sensitive child comfortable. If you have a shy child who wants you or a sitter to stay, you won't set her back in her progress by doing so. Keeping yourself in the background is one option. I frequently lent a helping hand to the host family or chatted with other mothers who stayed. I think, too, of two particular mothers who frequently stayed with me. Did we damage our children by staying? Well, none of us have raised children who are shrinking violets. One had his own radio show at the age of fourteen and interviewed, among others, then-President Clinton. The other boy just returned from a precollege trip to Tibet. My daughter has been interviewed by the media frequently because she's run her own business since the age of twelve. An armchair analysis might indicate that by staying when it was appropriate, we gave these kids added confidence in who they were and what they could be.

The "Only Mommy Do It" Child

Sometimes clinginess takes on the guise of the child gluing herself to only one parent, often the mother. While there are many nights when it feels much easier to simply go ahead and let Dad do the dishes and Mom do the putting to bed, don't fully play into your child's game. This is a case where you need to remember you're the parent and you get to make the decisions.

Particularly for mothers who spend more of the day with the kids, getting child-care relief from Dad is a wonderful treat. From the mother's point of view, she can complete the dishes without anyone saying, "One more thing, Mommy," so it's awfully nice to let Dad do the heavy lifting at night. From the father's point of view, having time with the children is an important requirement for building relationships with them.

The easiest way to overcome the "Mommy do it" syndrome is to have rituals that Dad is in charge of. Maybe Mom will give the last good-night kiss, but Dad can do the bath and the story. Once a child understands that either Dad reads a story or there's no story at all, chances are that everything will settle down to a nice routine.

A child who starts out feeling hesitant in social situations may never be the one to dance on the tabletops at parties or lead the group in a conga line. Even so, you can teach that child to overcome shyness so that he or she can feel perfectly comfortable when giving a speech or attending a party.

CHAPTER 5

Whining, Talking Back, Bad Words, and the Silent Treatment

Bobby, age seven, had had a great week visiting his cousins, a family with three boys ranging in age from six to twelve. When his parents came to pick him up to return to their home one hundred miles away, they were aware that Bobby seemed older, slightly more full of himself, but definitely ready to return to his neighborhood to reunite with his summer gang.

The first night home, his dad went out to the porch to summon Bobby in from the impromptu basketball game the kids were playing in the neighbor's driveway. "Bobby, time to come in now. It's time to have dinner."

Bobby, usually a cheerful, cooperative child, shocked his dad as well as the neighbors with his reply: "Stuff it, Dad. I'm not coming in, and you can't make me!"

What to do? His father was shocked and furious—not to mention embarrassed to have his son respond in such a way. Acting on instinct, Bobby's dad went out to the driveway and silently took Bobby by the arm and led him back to the house. After a moment's struggle, Bobby gave in—he knew he'd stepped over the line.

Judy and her four-year-old daughter, Rebecca, came back from a tiring round of after-school errands. As they entered their apartment building, Judy saw that the elevator was just about to go up, and she tugged Rebecca along with her, running the last few steps and boarding the elevator just as the doors closed. As they got in, Judy greeted one of her neighbors, an older woman with a few extra pounds on her: "Hi, Marilyn, it's good to see you," and she turned to Rebecca, prompting, "Say hello to Mrs. Selwyn, Rebecca. You remember, she lives just above us."

Rebecca hung back behind her mother and then darted her head out long enough to say, "I don't want to say hi to the fat lady, and I won't!"

Blushing crimson, Judy erupted, "Rebecca!" As she turned to Mrs. Selwyn with apologies, the elevator doors opened at their floor. Judy and Rebecca hastily left the elevator.

From the moment our children are born, the sounds they make and the words they say are totally theirs—not at all under our control. The innocent infant gurgle during a religious service brings smiles to those all around. But bathroom talk from a four-year-old or talking back by an eight-year-old causes an increase in parental blood pressure and insulted or annoyed looks from those who hear. Here's what you can do when these types of bad behaviors erupt in your household.

Understanding the Cause

As with all unacceptable behaviors, you need to examine the cause. In general, children say appalling things when something is bothering them. They may be cranky because they are tired or hungry and lash out with words, or there may be other reasons, such as these:

- *Need for attention*—Unfortunately, when kids are feeling neglected, they often don't care whether they get positive attention or negative attention. They just want the focus to be on them.
- *Experimentation*—What happens when you say "doody" in front of Grandma or use a curse word at school? Whether we like it or not, kids are exploring their world in many different ways.
- *Media models*—Children in movies and the stars of television situation comedies are wise guys. That's what makes them funny. Until

you teach your child that you don't want to be living with your own little Hollywood wisecracker, you may find that your kids pick up from the media both language and attitude toward parents.

- *Unrealistic parental demands*—What can anyone do if an adult says something like, "Go to sleep now!" Little ones are equally flummoxed by commands that are too big for them to grasp. "Clean up this room" is meaningless to kids under ages seven or eight. They need specifics: "Please put the blocks in the bin and the books back on the shelf."
- *History of getting away with it*—If your child has whined and gotten her way, or sassed you and been allowed to do what she wanted while the family is visiting relatives, then prepare for a repeat performance.
- *Separation from parents*—Each and every day, children take baby steps away from us. Sometimes they use language to establish that they are, indeed, their very own persons.

Be a Good Role Model

When it comes to poor communication skills (whining, using bad words, talking back, and so on) parents need to be conscious of their own behavior. Does either parent use expletives when angry? If so, now is a good time to stop.

And even parents have been known to be immature in some of their verbal responses to issues that make them angry. For example, when a department store clerk makes a mistake that involves voiding the receipt and running through all your purchases again, are you likely to "give her a piece of your mind"? Yes, it's inconvenient to have to wait, and perhaps you'd like to ask the manager to take over so that you can pay and leave the store promptly, but yelling at a clerk ("How can you be so stupid!") will not speed her up (it will probably actually slow her down), and you're serving as a poor role model for your child.

Also consider how you and your spouse respond to each other when you disagree. Do you yell and scream? Does one of you give the other the silent treatment? The better you become at modeling how to discuss an issue on which you disagree, the more likely it is that your child will realize that whining, talking back, using bad words, or giving someone the silent treatment is not the way to achieve desired results. (See Chapter 3 for additional suggestions on helping your child manage anger.)

What to Do: The Basics About Whining, Talking Back, Bad Words, and the Silent Treatment

Whether the problem is whining, back talk, dirty words, defiance, or the silent treatment (each of which we'll discuss separately), there are several things to keep in mind in stopping these bad behaviors:

- Don't take it personally. Blowing up at your child won't correct the behavior, and it models another behavior that you don't want your child to copy.
- Don't lash back. Both you and your child need to calm down. If necessary, leave the room and come back. Respond calmly. It's far more effective.
- If you don't feel calm, wait to deal with it when you do.
- Try to explore what lies beneath what was said, which likely has nothing to do with you.
- Label what has happened, and explain that it is unacceptable.
- Offer alternatives if appropriate.
- If some form of discipline is necessary, withhold a privilege (see Chapter 2).
- Keep in mind that this behavior will come and go in different forms as your child experiments with behaviors and words.

Though children's verbal missteps can be irritating and annoying, take comfort in the fact that the behavior is totally normal. Every parent has a similar challenge. Part of your job as a parent is teaching your children to voice their needs and opinions clearly and respectfully. One of the reasons we see five-year-olds whining for what they want and nine-year-olds (or teenagers) sass back as a matter of course is that parents don't think of these behaviors as "dangerous." Your child isn't going to get hit by a car if the behavior continues, so parents make three major mistakes that prolong the duration of these bad habits:

1. Parents prefer to avoid a fuss when possible. If your four-year-old screams, "No, I won't wear that hat!" it's generally easier to pack her up for preschool—minus the hat on her head—than to have a big fight on the way out the door. Besides, you'll put the hat in her coat pocket, and the teachers will make her wear it at recess.

2. Parents overreact. Granted, defiant language or attitude from your child is embarrassing if you're with others, and it is downright infuriating almost every time. As is often the case, the parental request (such as wearing a hat to school on a cold winter day) is made out of the desire to take good care of the child; it's no skin off your teeth if she doesn't want to wear the hat. That said, overreaction doesn't work: yelling, "You will too wear that hat, young lady!" while trying to force the hat onto a child's head only sets the stage for future confrontations.

3. Parents laugh. Whether it seems cute to hear a toddler use a swear word unknowingly or you're responding to how ridiculous it is for your school-age child to be imitating a cartoon character who talks back, your laughter sends the wrong message.

Great Idea!

The most powerful words you can say to a child who is whining, cursing, or talking back are, "There is a nice way to say that. Please try again."

Whining

Any parent who has lived with—or visited a family with—a whiner knows the sound: "Mommmmmmeeeee. I don' wannnna go nooooooow. My feeeet hurrrrrt." And whining, perhaps more so than the other traits in this chapter, can easily become habitual. That whimpering, whiny, ever-increasing high-pitched tone can be put to use in the morning ("I don' wannnna go to schoooool") and at noon ("I haaaate mac and cheeeeese"), grow worse by dinnertime ("Whennnnnn will you have time to play with meeeeeee?"), and become almost unbearable by night (Can't I stay up just a little lonnnnnnger?").

Whining is most common in the under-six set. Children this age want to do more and more for themselves, but they become easily frustrated and often decide—rightly so—that you can help them out. Whining is used to get your attention, and the underlying need is often fatigue and always a call for attention. It usually works, so they use it once again. After a while, you have a full-fledged whiner in your midst, and it becomes an ingrained habit that is harder to break.

The best thing for a parent to do is to nip whining in the beginning. If it's too late for that, the following strategy is still your best plan of action. It may just take a little longer to bring about a behavioral change.

- *Define the behavior*—Amazing as it may seem, your child may not even be aware of his behavior. "Please stop whining," is your first step to begin to identify the sound you no longer want to hear.
- *Make a game of it*—As with so many things, children get the point in a pleasant way if you take the time to make a game of it. Consider some role-playing games with two of your child's stuffed animals. For the voice of Baby Dog, you can use your most annoying whine, to which Mama Dog can vehemently object. Then Baby Dog can experiment with all types of voices, letting your child be the judge of the moment when Baby Dog achieves a proper Asking Voice. Once the game has established the behavior you're looking for, you can quickly ask for your child to use his Asking Voice whenever he veers off into a whine.
- *Make eye contact*—Emphasize your "please don't whine" point by getting down to speak to your children at their eye level, then say, "If you ask for something in a pleasant tone of voice, I'll try to help you out."
- *Acknowledge feelings but set limits on behavior*—Acknowledge the validity of their request, and remind them how they need to ask for it. "I know you want to go outside now, but you need to ask me in your regular voice." If the request isn't something you are able or willing to do, then make a suggestion: "I can't take you to the park now because it's raining, so you need to stop whining. If you sit by me and do three of your puzzles while I make a phone call, I will read you a story."
- *Avoid triggers when possible*—If you usually go to the grocery store in the late afternoon and find that your child whines as you shop, experiment. If you take her Saturday morning, does she still whine? If the whining continues no matter what you do, you may have to leave her at home or ask your spouse to do the shopping for a time.
- *Cede some control when possible*—Often what children whine about is their feeling of having no control. It's often very easy to give them some of the decision-making power, and you'll find their cooperation

increases tenfold. Consider: "I would be happy to play a game with you, but I'm washing the lettuce for dinner and still need to make your lunch. Would you like to do one of these chores so I can finish more quickly?"

- *Praise your child as you observe a change*—"Well, of course, I'll come out and throw the ball with you! You asked so nicely. I really appreciate hearing that tone of voice." You can even ask for tolerance—with praise: "I have to finish packing for my business trip, but you asked so nicely! I'll be happy to watch your dance just as soon as I finish." If she's impatient, you can give her a task such as getting a plastic bag from the kitchen that you need for packing, or suggest that if she practices the dance two more times, you'll have finished and will be in to see her by then.

So the whining is subsiding, and you're feeling better. Then trouble erupts. You're all out to dinner with Grandma and Grandpa, and you suddenly hear the beginning of a whine. Your son has decided to whine in public—a surefire way to get your attention. Don't cave in! If your child is incapable of talking in a "regular voice," then escort him away from the table so that the two of you can talk alone for a few minutes. Make your point in privacy.

Bad Words

Little kids who use bad language may be parroting something they've heard, picking up on the strength of the adult vehemence behind it rather than having any understanding of what they are saying. By preschool many children become quite interested in "bathroom talk." School-age kids may begin to hear true curse words on the playground.

Whatever they say and however they've learned it, the use of forbidden words takes on a mystique: "What will happen if I say it?" "I'm so grown up to be able to say these words." "Look at all the attention saying _____ gets me." "Dad says _____ whenever he's really angry. I will, too."

Note that sometimes children will accidentally use a racist or sexist term unknowingly. When you hear the type of word that is insulting to a particular group, stop your child by saying, "Do you know what that

"A torn jacket is soon mended; but hard words bruise the heart of a child."

—Henry Wadsworth Longfellow

means?" Often they won't. When told by a parent that a certain kind of comment would hurt the feelings of a friend or even a relative, most children will avoid the use of the term.

Washing a child's mouth out with soap or laughing at the preposterousness of such an ugly word coming from a young child will not achieve the results you want. Instead, follow these guidelines:

- Forbid name-calling of any type.
- Discuss why people use bad words, and explain why they aren't acceptable. Many of these words have very negative meanings, but some are just viewed by society as words that shouldn't be uttered by civilized people.
- If your child is at the age of enjoying bathroom talk, this is also a time when kids are fascinated with bodily functions. If the bathroom talk is generally discussed with friends, tell your child that adults—including you and the nursery school teacher—don't enjoy it.
- If your child is using a bad word in anger as a way of venting emotion, point out that the word chosen is a very unpleasant one and suggest that she choose a different, neutral one instead. People have been heard using words like "Sugar!" or a growl-like "Arrrgh!" in that way. Point out that by choosing her own "curse" word, she can select one that she feels is just right but one that won't offend the people around her.
- Some children continue their bad-word exploration by expanding their vocabulary. If you find that your child is trying more and more unsavory words, together make a list of all the words that are in poor taste. (Your child should provide the candidates for the list; there's no sense in giving suggestions for additional words to try.) That way you've been totally clear about the fact that these words aren't to be used.
- If bad language, name-calling, or the use of sexist or racist remarks continues, establish consequences. Be consistent in your follow-up.
- As the behavior subsides, offer praise.

Defiance or Talking Back

Sass. How dare they! For those of us raised by a generation of parents who would never have tolerated talking back, it is shocking when our child defies us. While parents are relatively understanding of the toddler's *Nos*, most of us become quite upset when this defiance continues and becomes insolent remarks such as "Why should I?" or "Try to make me!" or "You wish!"

In all likelihood, a young child is simply testing something he observed on television or a technique used by an older neighbor child. Your best plan is to remain calm and respond, "We don't talk that way. I know you don't want to stop playing, but we really have to leave now." Your child may give up the argument and come with you, but if not, you must follow through. A child young enough to carry should be picked up. With an older child, go to the child, take his arm gently, and lead him out of the room.

Children who sass must not get their way, and it's up to the parent to be certain that in this particular case, there is absolutely no negotiation. With an older child, you might add, "Jimmy, if you'd asked for five more minutes, I might have been able to give you a little more time. Because you've talked back, I feel angry, so we need to leave right now."

Use the following guidelines to correct this behavior:

- If your child is normally polite, simply say, "That's back talk, and it's not allowed." There is a good chance your child is experimenting and it won't happen again.
- Don't fight back, call the child names, or be sarcastic. The calmer and more matter-of-fact you can remain, the better the outcome.
- If the unpleasant talk continues, stop the conversation. Leave the room, saying, "I'm not speaking to you until you learn to speak nicely."
- Specify what the child said that upset you. "When you scream, 'It's not fair' at me, that makes me feel upset. We've been at the playground for two hours, and I think that's very fair. We need to go home now."
- Offer positive suggestions. A child who has this type of outburst is obviously angry, a very normal emotion. If the issue involves something like leaving the playground, then the remedy is relatively simple: "I know you don't want to go home. Rather than get so upset, next time why don't you come and discuss it with me? Sometimes we may really have to leave right away, but sometimes I may be able to

stay for a few more minutes when I see how important it is to you." At other times, something more may be going on. A child who talks back in the midst of a play date or right after school may be upset about something that has nothing to do with you. Try saying, "Mary, you don't usually talk that way to me. What was bothering you today when you came out of school? Maybe I can help."

- Offer coping methods. If your seven-year-old starts stomping around, saying, "I won't go!" when it's time for the family's regular visit to see his great-aunt in the nursing home, you might suggest strategies. (These types of coping methods help us throughout life whenever we have to do something we don't want to do.) You might say, "Aunt Sarah really loves seeing you, so it's important that you go, but let's think of what might make the afternoon more fun for you." Your suggestions could range from planning activities to do in the car to suggesting that a friend can come along, or letting your child pick the restaurant where you stop for dinner on the way home. The same type of method can be used for the child who is reluctant to go to the dentist or the doctor. There's nothing wrong with offering a simple treat after the visit or appointment. As adults, we frequently make deals with ourselves: "Well, if I get my filling done tomorrow, I'll treat myself to a milkshake for lunch because it will be easier than trying to chew something." We need to learn to set up little rewards for ourselves after accomplishing difficult tasks. This is how to begin teaching this system to our children.

- If the back talk or defiance has to do with a family responsibility such as putting clothing in the laundry or helping with dishes, make certain that the chore gets done. You can offer to pick up two pieces of laundry to his six or keep him company while he does the dishes, but kids need to understand that family members all help each other out. No classroom teacher will let your child get away with not helping; why should he get away with it at home? (Establishing this type of authority with your child is laying very important groundwork for the teen years.)

The Trial Lawyer Some families remark that their child's ability to argue makes the child well suited to being a trial lawyer, but sometimes they are misstating the case. The child who fights back isn't truly showing lawyerly qualities. A lawyer not only argues back but also listens to others and makes a strong case for herself.

Remember, too, the parent is both the opposing attorney and the judge. Even if your six-year-old makes a great case for staying up really late, you still know best. You can praise her presentation style and offer to listen to her in the future, but, otherwise, maintain the bedtime you know is best.

Families where children feel free to approach a parent with a well-reasoned argument tend to be very healthy families. However, even in these "democracies" where everyone feels free to speak up, there are occasions when parents have to have the final say. If you have a situation where you have to rule, state what the circumstance is and note that it is not open for discussion: "The Johnsons' invitation to take you with them to the movies was lovely, but your cousin is visiting this afternoon, so I need you here. I'm sorry, but this isn't open for discussion. Timmy will invite you again, or another time you can invite him to go bowling with us."

If your child is showing an interest in developing his negotiation skills, set ground rules: No raised voices, no name-calling, and each of you must have an opportunity to present your point of view.

If you find that your child calmly presents a well-reasoned case for a later bedtime or more television time, then you are going eye-to-eye with someone for whom you ought to start a law school savings account.

Rude or Hurtful Remarks As the family walked into the dining room for dinner, Lucy's mother was horrified when she heard her five-year-old say, while pinching her nose, "I don't want to sit by Grandpa! His breath smells bad."

Young children are admirable for their honesty, but unfortunately, being honest isn't always socially acceptable. The out-of-the-mouths-of-babes comments frequently put parents in awkward situations. The best way to manage the circumstance at the time is to handle it directly: "Why, Lucy, that isn't nice to say! It hurts Grandpa's feelings. Here, come sit by me for now."

By remaining calm, addressing the bad behavior, and making certain that your child's behavior won't escalate into a tantrum about sitting next to Grandpa, you can probably glide through the situation until the two

Trouble Zone!

If your child continues to be defiant, you should talk to the school psychologist or your pediatrician. Some help from an outsider may make a big difference to both you and your child. It's important to straighten out these types of confrontations as early as possible. They set a bad precedent for your relationship with your child in the years to come.

At Wit's End

"There are two great injustices that can befall a child. One is to punish him for something he didn't do. The other is to let him get away with doing something he knows is wrong."

—Robert Gardner

of you are alone. Then talk about why it isn't proper to make hurtful comments about people. "Grandpa has dental problems and can't help his bad breath. When you comment on it, it hurts his feelings because he loves you. Next time you're with him, think about how his eyes dance when he sees you and how pleasant it is to hold his hand when you're going to the park. Then maybe his breath won't bother you as much."

Kids also use rude and hurtful remarks when they get angry: "You're dumb, and your ears stick out. I hate looking at you!"

Whether the comment is directed to you, a sibling, a friend, or a stranger, the best way to handle a first or second offense is matter-of-factly: "That hurts feelings. Our family doesn't talk that way." And whatever the child is mad about should now be totally nonnegotiable, even if you might have given in to a more reasonable plea for a few more minutes' play time or whatever the desire was.

If the behavior continues, never give in to the demands that are being made by your child, and warn that you will remove privileges. If it occurs again, start doing what you said you would.

The Silent Treatment and Toddler Tune-Out

Ignoring parental requests starts early: You ask your toddler to pick up her toys because it's time for bed, and she acts as if she never heard you—or giggles and laughs and runs the other way. For a toddler, ignoring you is actually developmentally normal; she's practicing a bit of autonomy with the person she loves the most. (Lucky you . . .) That said, if you tolerate it, you may have a problem later on.

Most toddlers can manage only one-step processing, so keep any instructions simple: "Please put your stuffed animals on the shelf." If the task is more complex, show her how you'll work together. This is hard for toddlers to resist, because they love being helpful. "Wow, we did that in no time because you were such a good helper!" will reinforce your approval.

Incentives also are a good motivator: "When you are in your pajamas and have brushed your teeth, we'll read a book together."

While it's best to avoid going head-to-head with a toddler, if you do ask for something ("please bring me the cup") and your toddler doesn't cooperate, then you need to follow through. That may involve going to the table and picking up your toddler and the cup so that it can be placed in the sink.

If older children give you the silent treatment, they shouldn't accomplish their goal. "I know you're upset I won't let you go out and play now, but you have a choice. The rest of the family is going to help with the cut-out cookies, and you can help us or simply feel sorry for yourself." When he does eventually come and join you (as he probably will), don't · comment on it negatively or make any sarcastic comments. Speak in a tone that demonstrates you're glad he came to join you: "Oh, just in time. I need someone to stir the frosting."

If kids don't get attention for remaining silent and if they are reminded that it is they who are making the choice, they'll hardly ever use this attention getter for very long. It's boring if no one will make a fuss.

It takes work and determination to teach your child to voice needs and opinions respectfully, but remember that it's worth it. How children learn to present themselves is a key to all aspects of success in life. From having good friends to doing well in school, the process requires positive communication skills.

CHAPTER 6

Aggressive Behavior and Bullying

$\mathcal{S}$ arah's mother took the day off work to take Sarah to a group interview and play session for children applying to private school. Imagine her humiliation when the head of the lower school came out into the hallway where parents were waiting and explained in private that the shrieks from the classroom were occurring because Sarah had bitten another applicant. And she hadn't stopped there. When a teacher intervened, Sarah bit the teacher, too. Sheepishly, her mom entered the classroom with the woman, and Sarah was excused for the day. (Sarah did not "ruin her life" that day, though her mom thought so at the time. Sarah was accepted at another school at a later date and did just fine.)

Zachary's mother was equally horrified at Zach's behavior. Every time she and her three-year-old went to the playground, Zach would get so worked up over something that he often slugged another child or grabbed objects when he wanted to take possession of them.

Eight-year-old Mary faced a different problem, which she shared with her mother one night. When she got to school, kids routinely teased her about her glasses and copied the way she walked. She often had trouble finding someone to be with at recess, and she just hated going to school.

Bullying is defined as *repeated* negative acts committed by one or more children against another. The negative acts may be physical intimidation (hitting, kicking, or being physically threatening), verbal aggression (name-calling or taunting), or psychological manipulation

Experts feel that cases of bullying are vastly under-reported. Only half of all kids tell a parent what is happening, and even fewer tell a teacher. Few adults catch bullies in the act because most aggression occurs at schools in areas where there is less supervision. For example, trouble is more likely to erupt on the playground than in the classroom.

(excluding a child from something or from the group). The bullies are perceived as strong, and the victims, of course, are viewed as weak.

A certain amount of bullying used to be viewed as a rite of passage. Schools did what they could about the most overt bullying but looked the other way on a lot of it. However, recent research in the United States and abroad has documented that bullying is a common and potentially damaging form of violence among children. Not only does bullying harm both its intended victims and those who bully, but it also affects the overall climate of a school and mars students' ability to learn.

Studies show that both the bully and the victim suffer short- and long-term consequences. Victims experience more physical and psychological problems and have difficulty outgrowing the role of the victim. They are more likely to suffer depression, poor self-esteem, and other mental health problems.

Bullies were once thought to use aggression because they feel insecure. Experts now say that this isn't the case, that bullies are tough kids who lack empathy and love control and power. Dominating others in the classroom or the playground satisfies their need for being the top dog. Bullies themselves are at risk for short- and long-term problems. They lack the ability to solve problems in emotionally healthy ways, and they are at risk for developing future problems with violence and delinquency.

Whether your child is a potential bully or a child on the receiving end of being bullied, this issue needs and deserves all parents' attention. (Almost all children are either bullies or victims at one time or another; it's the rare being who can slide through life unscathed.)

Understanding the Cause

Aggression is a normal part of toddler development. During these years, children's language skills are not well developed, they care deeply about being independent, and they have very little impulse control. If they think of acting out physically, they don't yet have the self-control to understand they need to avoid doing what they are considering doing. (How often have you felt like "wringing someone's neck" or "punching someone," but as an adult you know that civilized people just don't behave that way.)

Some children are more aggressive than others or take longer to tame their instincts, so pushing, punching, kicking, and some biting may continue until an older age.

Be a Good Role Model

Parents need to model good problem-solving techniques and demonstrate how to get rid of angry feelings when upset. You can help your child a great deal by commenting on what you're doing. For example, if you come home steamed about something at work, apologize beforehand: "I'm really sorry, but I got upset about something at work. I'm going to ask the baby-sitter to stay an extra half hour so I can go for a jog." Or, "I am so mad right now about something at work that I'm going to put on my tape and do yoga. Do you want to do it with me?"

When you're angry at your child, make sure your child is safe, and put yourself in time-out. Announce what you're doing: "I'm going to go to my bedroom and lie down for five minutes, because I'm so upset right now."

Parents should not physically threaten or hit their children. If you model aggression, how can you teach them not to do it? (For more on anger management for kids and adults, see Chapter 3. For a discussion of spanking, see Chapter 2.)

Even if you are a good role model for anger management, children may learn aggression from other people. The model from which your child picks up aggression may be a relative or even a character on a favorite television show. If you have an idea where the bad influence is coming from, limit your child's exposure to the role model, whether it is a person or a television program.

If limiting exposure is not practical (maybe your child is in a classroom where the teacher is a screamer), talk to your child about how you see the situation: "I know the teacher yells at you a lot, but I don't think she's really angry at you most of the time. Some people think they have to yell to get you to pay attention, but if you're doing what you are supposed to be doing, then just try not to let it bother you." While a really serious situation may merit that you visit the principal, kids can learn to do well when working with different personality types. In many ways

Great Idea!

Sometimes aggressive kids are working off excess energy. Make sure your child is busy and has ways to use up energy. This may help reduce bad behavior.

Did You Know?

According to child psychologist and parenting expert
Penelope Leach in an
advice essay on parent
center.com, there is no
such thing as "harmless
violence." She discourages
parents from providing
pillows or other objects for
walloping to "get the anger
out." She believes that
children need to find other
ways to express themselves
and other outlets for anger.
If your child hits someone,
she says, "Take his hands
and say: 'No hitting. I know
you're angry, but we don't
hit people. Hitting hurts.'"

these experiences prepare them for the workforce where you often hear,
"You can't pick your bosses."

What to Do: The Basics About Bullying

No matter what type of aggressive behavior has taken place—and
whether the person being aggressive is your child or someone else's—
there are some basic actions for adults to take:

- Respond quickly. Children who are acting aggressively are in a
  heightened emotional state, so they probably won't remember what
  they're upset about unless you can stop the action as soon as it begins.
- If you witnessed what happened, separate the aggressor from the victim or the group immediately. Tell him what he did was wrong. If you
  did not see what occurred, the first thing to do is to step in to prevent
  anyone from being hurt or to calm anyone who is upset. You will have
  to listen to all sides to see if you can determine exactly who was the
  bully and who was the victim.
- Most kids need a cooling-down period. Even a couple of minutes will
  help. Sit or stand by the aggressive child and let him watch what is
  taking place with the group and/or discuss what happened.
- Ask the aggressor why she did it. With a little one, you may need to
  help answer that. "I think you pushed Tommy because you wanted
  the bucket, is that right? Isn't there another way to get the bucket?
  Did you try asking for a turn?" Young children need help in understanding why they felt so out of control.
- Accept his distress. "Everyone gets upset, but there are better ways to
  solve your problem."
- Tell her she must apologize. With a child reluctant to do so, wait until
  her body language is less angry, and go up to the other child and say,
  "Mary is having trouble saying she's sorry, but when she's feeling
  calmer, I know she'll feel bad that she hit you." Rather than thinking
  of this action as speaking for her, think of it as setting an example.
  Someday she will realize how "babylike" she is if her mom or dad has
  to do the talking.
- With younger children the problem can often be solved by establishing the taking of turns or getting another shovel from your play-

ground supplies. Unfortunately, children often push, pinch, or hit because they want a faster turn on the slide or because they don't think it's fair that Sam thought of bringing an action figure to the playground and he didn't. You may need to be sensitive and creative. Waiting in line with your son at the slide may help him learn the patience required in taking turns. Or discussing future plans to bring his action figures to the playground next time may help him overcome his current distress.

- Provide children with appropriate strategies for accomplishing their desires. Asking for permission, asking to borrow, and trading a toy for use of another child's toy are all ideas you need to implant. There's usually nothing wrong with a child's desire; it's the method of achieving it that needs to be refined.

- Don't yell or hit a child or call a child "bad." These reactions simply teach that verbal and physical aggression are tools that can be used if you're bigger and older.

- Be consistent. If your child is having a bad day, you may have to give up your playground conversation with your friends and hover near where your child is playing to intervene whenever she becomes aggressive. (Parenting is a full-time job. Your consolation should be that the more time you spend now, the easier your parenting life will be later on.)

- Keep an aggressive child away from play or out of a game for a few minutes with the information, "You can go back and play with your friends if you play nicely." If the aggression continues, you may have to go home and try another day. Over time, your child will begin to connect that certain behavior receives negative attention from you and you remove him from the fun.

- Parents are frequently embarrassed by the aggressive activities of their children. Most other parents understand, and if your child has slugged a child he doesn't know in the grocery line, just go ahead and address the issue with your child so that he doesn't think it's OK to do mean things in situations when he thinks you might let it slide.

- School-age children who are aggressive are old enough to be told what behavior is expected of them. Whether you have a boy who is playing aggressively to rise in the male hierarchy or a girl who is busy excluding certain girls in order to increase her status in a group, you need to stay on top of what is going on and define for your child

At Wit's End

"If your sister hits you, don't hit her back. Parents always catch the second person."

—Michael, age ten

"You should never mess with a kid that beat you up once already."

—Dannie, age ten

Trouble Zone!

Most children go through a
time where they show some
signs of aggression. If your
child is aggressive more
often than not, or if you or
other children have actually
been frightened by your
child's behavior, talk to the
pediatrician. Your doctor
can advise you on whether
you need to consult an
expert about ways to
further help your child.

which behaviors are acceptable and which aren't. If you see your son
snatch another boy's hat, tell him to give back the hat, adding: "You
may not snatch each other's things." If you overhear your daughter
plotting how to avoid having another girl sit with the group at lunch,
talk to her about how this will make the other girl feel. While your
daughter needn't be best friends with a girl she doesn't like, heavily
discourage the act of group exclusion. It's unnecessary and very
painful to another child.

- Always acknowledge good behavior. Whether you have a successful
afternoon at the park or you hear from the teacher that your daughter is bullying less, compliment your child on that accomplishment.

The Biter

No matter how unpleasant and animalistic it is, biting is a very normal
type of aggression. Few mothers who nurse beyond six months emerge
without an experimental chomp from their infant. Toddlers bite experi-
mentally—exploring their world as well as testing for reaction—and out
of anger or frustration or as a response when they feel threatened.
Because they have not yet developed good communication skills, it is
their way of exhibiting a response to a situation.

Unfortunately, biting brings out the worst in those bitten—frequently
parents. And children who become known as biters are frequently ostra-
cized. They don't get play date invitations, and some are even asked to
leave day care or preschool. It's definitely a behavior you should put an
end to as quickly as possible.

Young children have more power in their jaw muscles than in their
arms, so the pain is real. This, added to the very indignity of being someone's lunch, makes parental blood boil. However, like all other remedies, the key to correcting this behavior involves remaining calm yourself.
Here's what to do:

Did You Know?

According to one study, 50
percent of toddlers in day
care are bitten three times
each year.

- Use a sharp, attention-getting "No!" followed by a stern "No biting"
the moment you are bitten or when you see another person bitten.
You can follow up by saying, "We don't bite or hit or grab. Please use
words."

- Place your focus on the person who was bitten. If a child bites for attention, she'll soon see that being the aggressor is not successful.
- Don't laugh. And don't ever tell a story about how "it was so funny when Jenny bit so and so . . ."
- Remove the biter from the activity. Remind her there are other ways to express her anger or frustration or to make her needs known.
- Once she has calmed down, ask what she was upset about.
- If biting happens more than once or twice, consider the situations that inspire biting. Does your child have trouble sharing? Does she get stressed out at playgroup? Just like anyone, she may need to have the pressure reduced and not continue with that particular activity.

If Your Child Is the Victim

If your child is fearful of going to school or hates riding the bus or reports some other concern, you might suspect bullying. Here are some ways to help your child:

- Tell your child that nothing he did caused the bullying.
- Work with your child on demonstrating self-confidence. (Bullies are good at picking likely victims.) Children who speak up, make good eye contact, and are capable of using a sense of humor have an increased chance of not being picked on.
- If the nature of the bullying involves exclusion, particularly in the kindergarten and preschool set, work with your child on ways to include himself (see Chapter 4). At this age, exclusion tends to be more a matter of "why not exclude this kid" than a purposeful method of ostracizing one child.
- Coach your child to walk away from a bully and his or her gang and to tell an adult what is happening.
- Avoid saying bad things about the bully. Condemn the specific action, not the child: "What do you think Robbie was thinking when he told you that? It certainly wasn't a nice thing to say." Unless you move frequently, there is a good chance that, particularly with girls, your child may one day be best friends with the bully. For this reason, it's important to keep an open mind. Kids can and do change.

Trouble Zone!

Parents often hear, "If your child bites you, bite back." Bad advice. Children don't associate the pain you may inflict on them with what they are doing to their victims, so the effort is meaningless. The only thing they learn from your bite is that biting is something that adults do sometimes, too.

At Wit's End

"Actually, the only memory I have of being a Cub Scout was trying to get my hat back. That was all I did. Run back and forth at my bus stop, going, 'Quit it.'"

—Jerry Seinfeld

Did You Know?

According to a recent survey of teachers, classmates, and bullies themselves done by Duke University, bullies are among the most popular boys in school from the fourth through the sixth grades. The victim suffers doubly: Not only is he being picked on, but he is also being excluded from the popular group.

- Role-play the circumstances. Help your child think of strategies and answers to the bully.
- Check with the teacher to be certain that your child has not been isolated to the point that she is all alone for much of the day. The child who is being bullied really needs a social connection during this time.
- Encourage your child in hobbies or special interests that she enjoys or in which she excels. Feeling more confident in other parts of her life may give her the strength to escape some of the bullying.
- Sometimes kids who are bullied at school are also victimized in some way at home. Consider your child's relationships with his siblings or neighborhood children. If you think he is learning victimization close to home, find a way to change or end any damaging relationships.

Adults should not let kids "work it out for themselves." Any child who is being bullied needs and deserves help. This doesn't mean you need to overprotect your child by walking him to and from school when you wouldn't normally do so. It does mean that someone needs to intervene to help the bully and victim create a new pattern in the relationship.

If You Think Your Child Is a Bully

Teachers may tell of incidents that make you concerned, or you may actually observe your child overpowering and picking on another child. Whether it's your son exhibiting physical aggression or your daughter excluding others from her social group at school, these children need parental guidance and attention.

Bullies need to learn about respecting the rights of others. Just as the parent of a biter must hover and supervise, so, too, should a parent of a bully. A bully needs to be caught in the act and offered correction. This sounds hard, but it often isn't. By age nine or ten, girls will have phone calls discussing exclusion of one girl or another, and boys will frequently be caught laughing or joking at the expense of one of the other kids. Nip these behaviors in the bud. Your child isn't "bad," she just needs you to remind her what's right.

Bullies need to learn empathy. This is a trait that develops over many years, not necessarily developing fully until the teen years, so it's not too late to start! Whether you're watching television together or telling about something scary that happened to someone else, point out to your children how someone else might have felt. By reminding her of a time when she felt terrible about something, you will begin to educate her as to what her negative actions do to others.

Because schools are learning how detrimental bullies are in the school environment, many have established programs to help reduce the behavior among the children. Call your PTA representatives to discuss with them whether they would consider bringing in this type of program.

Trouble Zone!

Children who are overly aggressive may need to be evaluated for oppositional defiant disorders or conduct disorders. (See Chapter 12 for more information.)

What About Teasing?

Lots of families enjoy teasing, and playful teasing that doesn't hurt feelings can be OK. However, keep in mind that teasing is a form of verbal aggression and is usually meant to make another person feel self-conscious, left out, or just generally bad. Teasing is very much a part of our culture, so you do want to bolster your child's confidence about handling it.

Teasing can often be ignored. The person doing the teasing may give up if it doesn't get the expected rise out of the victim.

Teach your child the art of reframing the comment. If a child has just been teased about wearing a purple shirt, he might say, "I'm glad you like my shirt. Maybe I'll wear it again tomorrow." Or accept the truth: "Yeah, I do have red hair. Thank you for noticing." If a child is teased at gym class because of being bad at softball, try a compliment: "You play really well. I wish I could hit the way you do." Again, if the victim doesn't get upset or excited, the teaser may lose interest.

Within the family, avoid all types of teasing that ridicule or put down someone else.

Aggressive behavior, bullying, and teasing are common but negative aspects of our society. The more we as parents can do to curb these behaviors in our children, the better their world will be.

CHAPTER 7

Fibs, White Lies, Cheating, and Taking Other People's Things

"My Daddy is the strongest man in the whole world."

"I did too see a real ghost on Halloween!"

"I've only had one cookie, so can I have another?"

"My tummy aches, so I don't think I should go to school."

"Honest, I didn't break the glass. I don't know who did."

"He started it!"

Those are just some of the maybe-not-so-truthful comments you'll hear from children. But let's listen in on some adults:

"We'd love to come another time, Aunt Sue. We're just very busy this month."

"I think I'll call in sick. I need a mental health day."

"What am I going to tell your mother about why we don't want her to visit next month?"

"I love the purple and yellow sweater you bought me for my birthday, honey."

"I can't tell Mary I broke the vase she gave me. It would break her heart!"

"One adult, one child—she's only eleven" (describing your twelve-year-old to the person at the movie theater's ticket office).

In our culture, honesty is a strange commodity. We pride ourselves on knowing the truth, but we often find that it doesn't suit our interests to tell it. After all, if Mary doesn't notice the vase is missing, there's no sense in getting into it. And why make things tense with Aunt Sue by telling her that her aversion to young children makes it very difficult for you to see her right now?

Another issue connected to honesty has to do with cheating. While we generally connect cheating with one student copying answers from another, the whole ethic of honesty and integrity begins much earlier than that. Consider taking turns and preschool board games as an early opportunity to introduce conducting oneself with fairness and honesty.

We also expect honesty with regard to possessions. For children, taking things that don't belong to them probably isn't the first step toward a life of crime and petty thievery. Rather, they are showing that they still have lessons to learn about ownership.

So what messages are we giving our children about honesty? Mixed ones, certainly. As parents we need to consider carefully how we handle matters regarding honesty. Honesty is the basis of effective communication and healthy relationships. Because we want to raise our children to be moral beings, the first goal for this chapter has to be recognizing the truth—whether it's the truth behind a potential fib or the truth about who really owns the ball.

Later on, we can teach our children about refining that goal so that they don't blurt out how they really feel about their cousin or what they think of the teacher's new glasses. And, of course, part of understanding honesty is recognizing the difference between what's mine and what's yours.

Understanding the Cause

Preschool children cannot yet distinguish truth from fiction. To them, their daddy really does seem like the strongest man in the world, maybe even the whole universe. And making up tall tales is a normal activity that young children greatly enjoy. Because their stories are amusing, they provide the whole family with enjoyment.

Until your child is age seven or so, you should encourage truthfulness but not worry about raising a pathological liar or a thief. At this age, children don't fully understand the difference. Therefore, lies come out for a number of reasons:

- *Wishful thinking*—That trip to Disneyland she's describing to everyone (but you never took) is her hope for the trip you'll take one day soon.
- *To get attention*—The bigger the whopper, the more the focus is on the child telling it. Children may also run lies as a bit of a test. What will Mom do if I say that I don't know who dropped all the cereal for the dog? As with the whopper, a child gets some satisfaction out of seeing what family drama evolves around the lie.
- *To avoid something disagreeable*—A lie may seem like a reasonable strategy, whether the child is claiming a tummy ache to avoid going to school or professing not to know who broke something to avoid getting in trouble.
- *To show bravado*—Yes, he really can pick up a whole building. Well, he could if you let him go to the gym to work out.
- *To give the easiest answer possible*—It isn't important to them—at the time. She really did forget where she put the costume jewelry you let her play with, so she responds with whatever pops into her mind: "I think Sarah took it into her room."
- *To get even with a friend*—If a friend did something mean or is suddenly in good graces with the teacher, a child may be quite consumed

with anger or jealousy and try to use a fib to get the other child in trouble.

- *To be the "good one"*—Lies that blame everyone else seem to make the liar the good child.

By the time a child is seven or older, he is old enough to know that truthfulness is important. If a child lies, you'll want to talk to him about what's going on. Is he afraid of an unreasonable reaction from you, from your spouse, or from a teacher? Is he lying to protect a friend or a sibling? If you can give him a sense of safety about telling the truth (that you won't overreact if he's done something wrong, for example), and he continues to lie, then you ought to get some help with the problem. Start with the teacher, the school psychologist, or your pediatrician for some guidance.

As with lying, stealing—taking something that belongs to someone else—is not done intentionally in the early years. If a preschooler's friend has a special marker she's always wanted, the preschooler may well carry the marker home from a play date. Until the age of seven or eight, children are not capable of fully comprehending the wrongness of taking something that isn't theirs. If an older child is stealing, you'll need to find out why. If you stress the importance of not stealing, and it continues, seek out the teacher, the school psychologist, or your pediatrician for advice.

Be a Good Role Model

Children give us many reasons and opportunities to consider our own habits, and all parents need to hold mirrors up to their own behavior when it comes to truthfulness and rightful possessions. Most adults tell white lies, untruths intended to save someone else's feelings: "I didn't want to say we just didn't want to come, so I told her we had other plans that night," or, "How could I tell him his haircut was bad? It's going to take a couple of weeks to grow it out."

Parents also lie about responsibilities. They try to pay the child fare for tickets by saying teens are younger than they are. They lie about returning merchandise by telling the store it was a gift instead of admitting that they bought the item themselves over a month ago. And they lie to get out of work: "I just can't go to work today, so I'm going to call in sick."

As for the unfortunate parental reassurance about shots not hurting, don't go there. Shots do hurt, and you want to make your child feel as though he can trust you to tell the truth.

Children pick up on all this. Unfortunately, you're going to need to pay full ticket rates for the teenage cousins you take to the movies, and you ought to work out a different plan with your boss so that you no longer need to call in sick when you're just busy or stressed out. To raise children who do the right thing, we need to do the right thing ourselves.

Does this mean you should start telling your mother-in-law what terrible taste she has in home decorating? Of course not. Silence can take you a long way through an awkward moment, and as your child gets older, you can explain the occasions when "little white lies" can protect another person. Of course, their birthday thank-you notes shouldn't say, "Thank you for the game, but I already have it," or, "The sweater you sent me was way too small, so we had to give it to my little brother." You can work with them on writing kindly notes that express

Did You Know?

Research indicates that children as young as first-graders can begin to understand the difference between out-and-out lying and a white lie that is designed to avoid hurting someone's feelings. Parents should try to keep white lies to a minimum—and explain to a child why they are not telling the truth about why they're not going on vacation with their brother and his six kids. But that's hard, so it's comforting to know that children become somewhat sophisticated in this area early on.

Trouble Zone!

If an older child is lying about one thing or another on a regular basis, discuss your concern with her. Maybe the lies all involve keeping her out of trouble, and she's fearful of punishment from you or her other parent. If you catch her telling a fib, stop her and address it at the time. Maybe she's just not paying attention to what is true and what isn't. She needs to know you care.

gratitude even for things they don't like or can't use. For example, your daughter might write, "Thank you for the game. It is one of my favorites." Or your son might write, "Thank you for the sweater. The color is really cool. Thanks for taking the time to knit it for me." This attitude—whether written or spoken—will help a child understand that if honesty is hurtful ("I hate your haircut!") it might be best if such an opinion goes unspoken.

As for keeping things that aren't ours, we sometimes keep things by oversight. Whether it's a videotape you borrowed from a friend or a library book that has been around the house so long you actually packed it and moved to a new household with it, it's important to start keeping a better track of these things and to accept the consequences when we realize our mistake. As for bringing pens and paper home from the supply closet at work, this is a perfect time to clean up your act. A child who witnesses this can't distinguish why it would be wrong to bring home other people's things from school.

What to Do: The Basics About Fibbing

There are several things parents can do to encourage honesty and discourage fibbing:

- Encourage the truth. If you're with your child when Billy hits Stevie and your child stands witness to the fact that it was Stevie who hit Billy, try asking again. "Are you sure that's what happened? I thought Billy hit Stevie." And if your child is hesitant to come forward to say who spilled something or broke something, reassure her with, "I won't be mad. Just tell me how it happened." Then live up to your word.
- Support your child when she tells the truth. "I'm so proud of you for explaining what happened today."
- Don't ask your child to lie for you. If a friend calls and you don't feel like talking, take the phone yourself and explain you'll call back.
- Don't call your child a liar, no matter what happens. That's a powerful word of condemnation.

- Don't ask no-win questions. The age-old parent trap goes something like this:

You: (*calling from downstairs to Lily, your seven-year-old, who is brushing her teeth*) Did you pick up the game in the family room?

Lily: (*thinking, "Well, maybe I did; I sort of pushed the pieces to one side"*) Yes.

You: (*entering the family room*) Lily! You did not pick up this game!

The more experienced you get at parenting, the better you'll do at avoiding no-win questions. Making beds, doing chores, and remembering to put away games are not important to kids. Your better approach would be to check the family room first (don't ask), and then make the request based on what you know: "Lily, I see that you didn't have time to pick up the game you were playing. Would you please come down and do that right now?" The extremely mature child may answer, "I forgot. I'll be right down to put it away." (But don't hold your breath.)

Sometimes it's appropriate to set consequences—such as a withdrawal of a privilege—for lying. Discuss your concern with your child, set the consequences, and follow through.

Imaginary Friends: Blurring Truth and Fiction?

Imaginary friends are very common among children between the ages of three and five. Pretend play with invented playmates may range from such simple interactions as building with blocks to complex fantasy play in which the playmate becomes an active family member. Eldest and only children are most likely to have imaginary friends, though any child who enjoys imaginary play could adopt one. When the imaginary playmate is ever present, parents worry that if they play along with the game, they are creating difficulty for their child in separating truth from fiction.

Did You Know?

Experts say that children who have imaginary friends tend to be happier in day-to-day activities, more verbally communicative, more cooperative, and less overtly aggressive. Not bad for a start!

Imaginary friends fill three primary roles: companion, confidante, and, often, scapegoat. It is the role of scapegoat that tends to worry parents most. "Mommy, some juice spilled in the kitchen, and I think it was Huey." While you might prefer your child to say, "Mommy, I spilled some juice in the kitchen," there's no harm in blaming Huey. In this case, your child aligned himself with you, and you can enlist his aid: "Oh, Huey must have been too sad to tell me himself. I'm glad you told me, though, so we can clean it up before the floor gets sticky. After we mop it up, then maybe you and Huey will share a second glass." This response paves the way for the lesson that you're not going to yell or punish poor clumsy Huey, but you are going to praise your child for reporting the problem, which in a way was telling the truth. (He could have gone off and played in his room, letting you discover the spilled juice later.)

Children frequently use imaginary friends to work through fears and concerns. This is particularly clear if your child creates a nighttime friend who is good at scaring away monsters, for example.

So if it's OK to add an imaginary child to your family, how far should a parent go to respond to it? Here are some guidelines:

- Take your cue from your child. Some friends are private affairs. Your child may mention the new pal but never seem to bring the imaginary friend anywhere with you, including the table at mealtimes.
- Even if you're entranced by your child's creation, remember it's your child's friend. Don't add to the game or become too involved, or the friend will no longer serve the purpose for which your child created him.
- You can sometimes talk things out through the game. If Huey is beside himself over starting a summer camp program, this allows you to discuss with your son some of the things he could tell Huey to help him feel better.
- If your child does want to bring you into the game, follow your instincts. If you don't mind a placemat being laid for the friend at dinner but adding a chair crowds the table, then set your boundaries: "Can't Huey sit in your lap? If we add a chair, I can't get by to clear the table." When you're out, you can say, "I don't think Huey could

eat a whole ice-cream cone by himself. Let's buy you one, and then you can give him bites of yours."

- Even if you think imaginary friends are dumb, don't say so. A comment like, "Oh, stop making that up," does a lot of harm. Children can develop useful skills from playing with imaginary friends. Fantasy play is great for the imagination and offers children an opportunity to work out everyday stresses. The little boy who ratted out Huey for spilling the juice learned that his mother would not have punished him for the spill and, in fact, appreciated being told and included him in the adult responsibility of cleaning it up.

- Visit the library and ask for some storybooks that involve imaginary friends. These books tend to place imaginary friends in perspective. You and your child will probably enjoy them.

- Imaginary friends tend to disappear when they are no longer needed—after the anxiety of the first day of school is over or a few months after the completion of a family move.

Trouble Zone!

Imaginary friends are a problem only if a child becomes so preoccupied with the friend that he or she isn't interested in being with real children. If your child goes through more than a few days of this type of obsession, check with the teacher or call your pediatrician for advice.

What to Do: The Basics About Cheating

When your child is born, school—and the possibility of what we classically think of as cheating—is a long way off. However, parents lay the groundwork of teaching children not to cheat in a child's early years.

As children go through toddlerhood with a focus on "me" and "mine," this self-focus gets played out in games with cries of "Me first! Me first!" With little ones, we're inclined to go along with this directive, letting a two- or three-year-old have her way when we start a game or set up a system on the swing set to decide which sibling goes first. However, as soon as you can, start teaching your child the concept of fairness in game playing.

- Board games are a particularly good opportunity for teaching some life "rules." Although sitting through yet another game of Candyland or Chutes and Ladders tests the patience of most parents, think of it as a Golden Opportunity. Yes, he can take the first turn on the first game. When you play the game again, you get to go first. Can he take two turns in a row? Absolutely not. Can he skip ahead a little so he misses the chute that he was supposed to land on? Nope. Teaching kids to observe the rules of a game helps prepare them for everything from fair play on the playground to rules of order in the classroom.

- Sometimes no one can tolerate a long, drawn-out game. If bucking the rules seems to be the order of the day, pronounce the game as such: "Let's play the New Rule way. We'll make up the rules as we go along." That way your child doesn't have to think of board games as an intense time where Mom or Dad preaches about fairness. You've created some wiggle room for doing what kids do best—acting funny and silly.

- Observe play among siblings or with friends. A determined child may somehow arrange for all the turns to be hers, despite paying lip service to taking turns. Parents need to monitor these occasions to be certain that no cheating is going on.

- Parents usually don't need to preach about not copying other children's work when their children are in the early elementary grades. Teachers will explain the importance of "doing your own work." As your child gets older, you will be able to discourage your child from "calling John for the answers in math" and the sorts of things that you hear about around the household.

- If you do observe or hear about early cheating in school, talk to your child about it. From the beginning, it's important to convey to a child that school is about learning, not about doing everything perfectly. (See "What's Wrong with Perfection?" in Chapter 8.) Children need to hear again and again that you want the work to be theirs, not someone else's.

What to Do: The Basics About Stealing

Young children have little sense of ownership. Under the age of four, everything is "mine," and it's very difficult for a preschooler to curb impulses. Somewhere between the ages of five and seven, children develop a hazy notion of wrongness and begin to learn honesty. Here are some ways to help them learn:

Great Idea!

This one may not feel like a great idea, but you'll reap the rewards for years to come!

It's 5:15 P.M. You get home from work and discover the sitter forgot to pick up milk, so you load everyone into the car for a quick trip to the market. After waiting in line for six minutes with two grumpy kids, you finally pay for the milk and leave the store. Just as you step outside, holding hands with the kids and struggling with the change because you didn't take time to put it in your wallet, you realize the clerk gave you too much change.

What to do? Make the unplanned and unexpected expedition into a memorable lesson. Kneeling down, you say to the kids, "Look, the lady gave me thirty-five cents too much in change. We're going to take it back."

- You can begin to establish early lessons with something of yours and something of your child's. Each of you holds one possession and then trades, identifying which is Sylvie's toy and which is Daddy's ruler, for example.
- If your child comes home with a toy from another home, ask about it. Chances are, you'll be told, "Sammy let me." Check with Sammy's parent—maybe he did, or maybe he did and doesn't remember. At early ages, giving away toys is common, but it usually doesn't work out well because the giver often forgets she said she didn't want it anymore. The best solution is to discourage trading or giving at these ages. (Taking turns with a toy during a play date should be encouraged; giving or accepting a toy on a permanent basis is different.)
- Never let your child keep what he stole. Show disapproval if your child takes something, and let your child know you take it seriously. If your little one comes home with a candy bar from the rack at the checkout counter, express your concern: "Wow. I didn't know you had this. We can't ever take anything from the store without paying. I'll have to take it back." Then you'll have to do so, no matter how insignificant the item and how annoying the trip back to the store—it's that important.

- Discuss the feelings of others. While it's difficult for a child to understand that a drugstore with racks and racks of candy bars will miss one, she can begin to understand that if she takes a marker from her friend's house, her friend won't have it when she wants to use it.
- A good way to explain not stealing is to tell your child, "In our family we have a rule that we don't ever do that." This behavior deserves a tough stance, and explaining it as a rule generally helps a child better understand the concept.
- Over time children need to understand that money has ownership and has to be earned. It isn't available to just anyone who sticks a card into a machine at the bank.

Life lessons taught early really stick. When you take the time to do the right thing, you'll be well on your way to raising kids with all the right stuff inside them.

CHAPTER 8

Daily Dilemmas

Inspiring Good Behavior When You Need It

The previous chapters help you with the behavior biggies, but there are still a lot of things that can go wrong during the day. Here's some quick advice on what to do about some specific problems (the car seat tantrum, problem behavior at the mall) and specific habits (dawdling, thumb sucking).

Bad Behavior in the Car

It's raining, traffic is bad, and you're late getting the kids to school. As you drive, your kids and the neighbor child are having a rip-roaring fight. What to do:

- Try a verbal warning. It can't hurt.
- If the kids ignore your warning, then pull the car over to the curb or the side of the road and turn the motor off.
- Explain to the children that the car will not start again until they are quiet. If a "he said, she said" discussion ensues, explain that you will discuss this with them later, but right now everyone needs to be quiet so that you can take them to school.
- Do not drive until they have modified their behavior.

- Keep age-appropriate amusements in the car, and be prepared to listen to children's music instead of radio news. Backseat peace is worth not being up-to-date on what's happening in the world.

The Car Seat or Seat Belt Tantrum

The nice thing about state laws is that the safety behavior you need is actually something a police officer would enforce. Here's how to do your part:

- Explain to your children that the seat belt or car seat rule is a rule for everyone in the country.
- Point out something fun you're going to do as a result of going out in the car that day.
- Tantrums often come because children want to feel in control. Try to go to the car early enough that you can let your little one get into his car seat and do as much of the belting as possible before you need to fasten the safety catch. This lets children feel more in charge of their confinement.
- Car seats can get extremely hot; some children resist getting in the seat because of the memory of a bad experience. Cover the car seat during summer months, and always check it before encouraging your child to sit down.
- Some children have tender tummies. A child who fights car rides may get carsick but be too little to explain to you that his stomach bothers him in the car. While there's not much you can do for short car trips, discuss with your pediatrician what remedies to use for longer car or plane rides.

Thumb Sucking, Nose Picking, Nail Biting, and Other Bad Habits

Whatever the bad habit, the basic approach to breaking it is the same:

- Identify the habit you would like your child to break, and discuss why it's a bad habit. (Nose picking spreads germs to himself and to others;

thumb sucking looks babyish and is bad for his teeth; nail biting is germy, and so on.)

- Together talk about a time when it might be easier to break the habit. Don't ever try to break a habit at times of stress, such as the beginning of school.
- Consider reminders. A string tied around a thumb or around the nose-picking finger may help remind your child to make a change.
- Are you willing to provide motivation? If you use an accomplishment chart and mark successful days, what are you willing to provide after a certain number of days when your child has accomplished the goal?
- Are there alternatives to the habit? Instead of sucking his thumb or picking his nose, maybe there is a craft activity he could learn so that his hands are busy while watching television.
- Consider what triggers the habit, and try to avoid it for a time. Does your child primarily pick his nose when watching TV? If so, try to keep your child more active for a few days in order to break the habit.
- Sometimes peer pressure will cause your child to give up a bad habit.
- An outside professional is often your best ally. The doctor or dentist who hands your child his business card with the offer of helping him give up the habit may provide just the motivation your child needs to kick the habit.
- Praise the child who makes the effort to quit, and be effusive in your praise of the child who actually succeeds.

The Annoyance of Interruptions

"Mommy, mommy, mommy, mommy!" What more needs to be said? Sometimes it seems that being constantly interrupted is woven into the fabric of the parent's life. Here are some suggestions for discouraging this behavior:

- Young toddlers are almost incapable of waiting; their mental development literally cannot factor in that anything else could take your attention. However, they can sometimes be diverted. Try to do activ-

At Wit's End

"There are three ways to get something done:
1. Do it yourself.
2. Hire someone to do it for you.
3. Forbid your kids to do it."

—Anonymous

ities like phoning at times when they are napping, or save special things to occupy them when you need to get something done. An activities bag reserved for such occasions or special permission to watch a videotape will usually buy you a little time before they think of needing you again. A cordless phone or a cell phone can also help, because you can be where they are actively involved.

- Preschoolers are a little bit better at waiting, and it's important that you start helping them develop this ability. Expect your preschooler to be able to wait no more minutes than he is old. A three-year-old should be able to wait three minutes, for example.

- If your child interrupts you, explain what you are doing and that you need her to wait for three minutes.

- If she becomes agitated and starts crying or screaming, say, "I still need you to wait. You need to calm down. You'll have to explain what you're saying in your nice voice."

- Don't scream at your child or threaten. Warning, "If you interrupt me one more time . . . ," doesn't teach anything.

- School-age children are definitely capable of waiting a few minutes for your attention. Expect them to do so. They have to in class.

- After your child has waited, be sure to remember that she was waiting and say, "Thank you for waiting. Now how can I help you?"

- Be conscious of your own behavior. When you need your children to leave a game or stop doing something they are enjoying, or if you have to cut off your talker in midsentence, say, "I'm sorry to interrupt you."

The Grocery Store and the Mall

Shopping with children is challenging but not impossible. These guidelines will smooth the experience:

- Before starting out, state the terms of the trip, along with your expectations. Information might include the number of stores at the mall you need to visit or the type of groceries you need to shop for.
- If you can afford the time, promise a special activity (for example, lunch out, stopping for ice cream, or purchasing one special thing of the child's choosing at the grocery store) at the end of the trip. "If you help me so that I can get everything done, then we'll _____."
- State any rules you know your child needs (no touching the merchandise, no loud talking, no running in the store, and so on).
- Create an age-appropriate job for your child, and tell her about it. A toddler can hold the grocery list or help pick out the kind of cookies you'll have for this week. A preschooler can fetch same-aisle groceries for you; a school-age child can read the list and keep track of what you've accomplished.
- If the trip goes well, be sure to deliver on your special treat. Tell your children how much you appreciate their help.

The Doctor and the Dentist

Going to the doctor or dentist is scary for most of us, so remember that stress management is part of your challenge in achieving good behavior. Try these strategies:

- Check out library books about visits to the doctor or dentist.
- Try to book appointments early in the day so that your child isn't worn out before you even arrive.
- Discuss why you are going and what will happen.

- Don't tell children that something won't hurt when it will.
- Take activities with you to occupy your child. She may enjoy the toys in the waiting room, but once you're in the examining room, you may still need something to do.
- Doctors and dentists who discuss things directly with your child are ideal. Be sure to include your child in age-appropriate aspects of the discussion.
- Think of what might make some difficult visits fun. When my youngest daughter had to have major surgery when she was eight, we took a camera with us to all the pretesting and photographed my daughter and the medical professionals involved. Afterward, we created a storybook about her experience. The project helped provide fun during an unpleasant activity, and the book she created was helpful to her—she read it again and again. She also took it to school with her and was able to explain to her classmates what she had been through.

At Religious Services

Attending a religious service with a child requires patience on the part of the parent and cooperation on the part of the child. Your actions can help develop cooperation:

- Explain where you are going and what will happen. If your child is wearing different clothing for the occasion, explain why. Even people who attend services regularly should explain to their children more than once what the experience is all about.
- Talk about what kind of behavior is necessary.
- Talk about strategies you yourself use when you're having trouble sitting for a long time. (Can you take anything along for your child to do?)
- Discuss with your child what is permissible if he just can't sit any longer.
- If children attend all or part of the adult services (as opposed to going to a class), you will likely need to take your child out for a time. You and your spouse can take turns at this if the service is long.

- If your child is disruptive, leave with her. This is not the time to make a point about good behavior.

Motivating the Dawdler

Some children are dawdlers from birth. Others go through stages when they endlessly dawdle. Whether you have a lifer or your child is simply going through a phase, here are some suggestions:

- Begin by planning extra time for "dawdler management." You may have to get up earlier or reduce the number of things you expect to accomplish before leaving home.
- Build in dawdling time for him or her as well. Your dawdler may need forty-five minutes for breakfast, so plan for it.
- Provide your dawdler with a clock. You might try placing a clock radio (set to an upbeat station) on the other side of the room to help your sleepyhead get out of bed.
- Have breakfast ready so that after the dawdler is dressed, he or she can go immediately to the table.
- Eliminate distractions. Morning television and playtime should be permitted only after a child is dressed and ready for the day.
- Countdowns in five-minute increments help everyone prepare for a transition. (For the true dawdler, five-minute warnings may need to start fifteen minutes ahead.) Combine countdowns with task reminders for the younger child: "Five minutes until we leave. Please go to the bathroom now."
- Motivate your child to be ready to leave in time by reminding him or her of something pleasant that is to happen that day. "Time to leave for school now, and remember, you have library today!"
- Reminding your child that if she is late she will have to walk into the classroom after everyone is settled can be a great motivator.
- Take over. Some mornings, you may not be able to allow her to tie her own shoes or pour her own milk. Spell out those rules ahead of time, so that the change of power doesn't have to be carried out in anger. "If you're ready on time, you may tie your own shoes. If we're running late, I'll need to help you."

- For the born dawdler, reward systems can sometimes help motivate habit change. Consider stars on a chart, a penny reward, or the promise of a special game in the evening for every time a dawdler is ready to leave on time.

What's Wrong with Perfection?

Adults frequently forget that the problem with perfection is that it's impossible. The child who sets herself up to do things perfectly is doomed. She'll encounter heightened frustration and may suffer all her life if she doesn't learn early on that trying your best is good enough. Here are ways to ease the pressure on your child:

- Talk about how everyone makes mistakes, and point out the times when you goof up.
- Point out the value of trying rather than succeeding.
- Encourage relaxation in your child's approach to life. *It's no big deal* are good words to use with your child when Cheerios spill or when you have to iron a shirt again.
- When something goes wrong, teach your child to ask, "OK, but can it be fixed?" The perfectionist may want to destroy an imperfect math paper or a drawing that doesn't live up to his standards. Show ways to fix the mistake by erasing, using correction fluid, or easily making a correction on the computer.
- Emphasize flexibility. Perfectionist children have difficulty coping with something they didn't anticipate. When plans get changed, talk through your own disappointment and be sympathetic with your child. Then together find something good about the change that has happened. Because it rained and you couldn't go on a picnic, you got to go to a movie instead, for example.
- Don't model a perfectionist attitude yourself. It's useful for your children to see that when you bake chocolate chip cookies, they don't always come out, and when you're building something, you sometimes have to take some nails out and start again. They learn through your example.

Bad Behavior from a Child Not Your Own

Don't be afraid to enforce your house rules with a playmate who is visiting. Explain as many rules as necessary in a positive light. "We eat snacks in the kitchen. We don't carry food with us around the house."

If another child is misbehaving at your home, don't yell or get upset. Simply step in and explain what the house rules are. Often the "class bad kids" can behave quite well at the home of someone whom they come to respect.

PART THREE

Encouraging Good Behavior

CHAPTER 9

Mealtimes

The ideal mealtime provides a wonderful opportunity for family members to bond and for parents to model appropriate behavior. But if you're a normal family, your mealtimes are more like this:

"Dinner time," calls Mrs. Smith as she finishes preparing the family's spaghetti dinner after arriving home from work. Mr. Smith has just walked in the door and tells her, "I'll be right down." There is no response from four-year-old Amy, who is playing with her dollhouse, or Jack, eight, who is watching TV.

Mrs. Smith puts everything on the table herself and goes to the family room to physically prod the kids into coming to dinner. "Have you washed your hands?" When the answer is no, the two go off to wash their hands together, and Jack gives Amy a shove on the way. Amy shrieks. "Kids, stop it!" warns Mrs. Smith. The phone rings, and the dog starts barking to come in.

Once at the table, Amy looks at the spaghetti and whines, "I don't wannnnt spaghetti tonight." Jack dives into the spaghetti with the comment, "Shut up, Stupid." Amy bursts into tears, gets out of her chair, and goes and buries her head in Mrs. Smith's lap. "Tell him to quit being mean to me!" she sobs.

Soon Mrs. Smith is up getting something different for Amy to eat, Jack has already done justice to his serving of spaghetti but announces, "I'm not tasting that vegetable—it looks gross!" He takes a piece of bread, eating only the insides and creating little crumbs with the crust, many of which fall on the table and are brushed to the floor.

Mr. Smith comments, "Can't we just have one family meal when everyone comes to the table and eats what's there without whining?"

By this time, Mrs. Smith has returned with a plate of noodles for Amy, and in exasperation, she sits down to eat her now-cold spaghetti. Jack asks to leave the table, and Amy soon follows.

This isn't a true horror scene—that would involve a crying baby and a toddler throwing her bowl and spoon from the high chair. But it's certainly not the type of family dinner that would make it into a television show featuring the ideal American family.

That said, there is great hope for the Smiths. With a little tweaking of their current family practices, they could have a pleasant meal where everyone eats what is served and they have the energy for a decent family discussion. Here's how.

Mealtimes Require Transitions

Making a smooth transition from one activity to another increases the odds of better behavior when starting the new activity. Mealtimes are no different. Even if Mom or Dad is serving your favorite food, would you like to be dragged in from playing with your friends or be told to turn off a television program in which you've already invested twenty-two minutes and not get to find out how the comedy ends? To minimize the problem, follow these suggestions for the transition to mealtime:

- If it is possible to establish a regular mealtime, this greatly aids the family transition to the table. Kids become familiar with the rhythm of the evening, and they are more willing to break away from their activities if the meal is held at the same time each day. While sometimes families have to eat at different times on some evenings, this schedule change increases the likelihood of fatigue and hunger interfering with the children's ability to behave at the dinner table. Experts say little children who are fed on an erratic schedule actually worry about whether or not they will be fed.
- A quiet activity before dinner generally makes the transition easier. School-age children might work on their homework at the kitchen table while you're in the kitchen, or younger children might be given puzzles or encouraged to play with Legos, a dollhouse, or blocks before dinner. Watching a bit of television before dinner is fine, too,

but don't let your child start a new program at 6:00 P.M. if you're hoping to eat at 6:15 P.M.

- Give a five-minute warning before you need everyone at the table. Have everyone wash up at that time and come to the kitchen as soon as they have done so.
- Give children age-appropriate responsibilities for taking things to the table.

Great Idea!

If you are the main cook, remember to ask someone to help with cleanup!

Family Members Who Help with Dinner Behave Better

The 1950s image of Mom in the kitchen in her apron lingers with us even today, and in too many households, the expectation is that Mom will fix dinner. Why? With the high number of working mothers, why is dinner viewed as a female responsibility? Men who lived alone before marriage found some way to feed themselves, and from the age of three up, children can be very good helpers. Family participation is key to the success of the family meal because all who have participated in bringing about an event—in this case, a meal—are more invested in having it work out well. Here are some ideas that might help you figure out how to get everyone involved:

The parent who is home first is a good candidate for taking primary responsibility for meal preparation. The other parent can cook on weekends, take responsibility for grocery shopping and/or meal planning, or be responsible for cleanup.

Ask your children to help with tasks they can learn to manage themselves. The younger the child, the more excited he'll be at being asked to be your helper. In the beginning, teaching children what needs to be done may seem to take more effort than it's worth, but over time, the payoff is enormous. (When my girls first started helping me make holiday cookies, we made three types, and it took us a day and a half. Imagine my shock one year, when we did the entire process in about two and a half hours!)

- A three-year-old is capable of one-step tasks. She could wash lettuce by bringing a chair to the sink and working beside you. She is capa-

ble of setting the table, though you might need to break the tasks into parts: first the napkins are put at each place, then the forks, then the knives, then the spoons. If any cool dish needs to be stirred, three-year-olds are good at that, too.

- A four-year-old can add to the preceding tasks the ability to wipe the table before setting it. A four-year-old also can pour premeasured ingredients (and be introduced to the concept of measuring) and peel, spread, roll, and mash foods.
- By age five, a child can make a simple breakfast or lunch. However, if the toaster or microwave is involved, you should be there to supervise or take over when anything has been heated. Five-year-olds can also measure and grate and grind foods. They may even be able to cut if you've had time to teach and supervise for a while.
- Older children are fully capable of doing a great deal to help with dinner preparation. Start training them early, and you'll be surprised at how much lighter your burden is.

A benefit to enlisting help with dinner is that it assures you everyone will be nearby and ready to sit down when the meal has been prepared.

The Food Itself

"I don't like meat loaf," whines your four-year-old. Those are annoying words to anyone who has just fixed dinner. You certainly don't want your child to leave the table hungry, but you should avoid becoming a short-order cook. Here's what experts recommend:

- Offer choices and an interesting variety when possible. In addition to a basic dinner, provide child-friendly foods such as bread or a bowl of pasta. Even if your child doesn't like the main course, there will be something already on the table that he will eat.
- For new foods or foods your child professes not to like, serve a small portion. Tell your child she is expected to try it, taking at least one bite. Nutritionists say that children may have to be exposed to a new food fifteen to twenty times for it to become one they like.

- Eating jags are normal for kids. The child who will eat only peanut butter and jelly sandwiches for three months may suddenly switch to macaroni and cheese. You can check in with the pediatrician if you think your children may be missing something nutritionally, but most of the time, their eating averages out healthfully enough over time.
- Keep in mind that appetites vary for each child. When children are going through a growth spurt, they'll eat more. They'll be less hungry when their growth slows down.
- Young children prefer not to have their food mixed. If you're serving pasta with something on top of it, it's simple enough to serve your child the two foods on different sides of the plate, even if everyone else has their pasta and sauce served together.
- Never force a child to eat once she is full. All family members should be encouraged to stop eating when they have had enough. No one should be forced to "eat just a little more" or to clean her plate.
- Children need to learn early on that food is nutrition and fuel—not a way to treat yourself better or comfort yourself when you're down. Using food for rewards and comfort increases the likelihood of eating disorders. Food should not ever be used as a reward, and food shouldn't be used as comfort. If your child had a big disappointment, don't use the feeling as a reason to go out for ice cream.
- Adults need to model good eating habits. Kids mimic what they see, so if you enjoy experimenting with different foods, chances are good that eventually your children will, too.
- Don't reward or threaten with dessert, by saying such things as, "No dessert until you've eaten your vegetables." A small sweet such as a cookie or a piece of fruit can be offered as an expected part of a meal.

At Wit's End

"Children measure their own life by the reaction, and if purring and humming [are] not noticed, they begin to squeal; if that is neglected, to screech; then, if you . . . console them, they find the experiment succeeds, and they begin again. The child will sit in your arms if you do nothing, contented; but if you read, it misses the reaction, and commences hostile operations."

—Ralph Waldo Emerson

Teach Good Manners

Age-appropriate good behavior should be expected at dinnertime, and though toddlers are messy and preschoolers are tired by dinnertime, it is still possible to establish a system of civilized behavior at the table. Sometimes families find it necessary to establish table rules such as no scolding, no fighting, and no audible bodily noises (such as burping) while having dinner.

Good manners are helpful in making friends and sailing easily through life, and dinnertime offers the perfect opportunity for all family members to practice manners. While nagging throughout dinnertime is a guaranteed way to ruin the family meal, parents can teach many social niceties that are often needed during a mealtime simply by setting a good example. Here are some additional ideas for teaching table manners:

- Children should learn early that they may not beg for bites of someone else's food, eat in a disgusting way, or make bad noises at the dinner table.
- "Please" and "thank you" are easy to use throughout a meal as family members pass items back and forth.
- Children can easily be taught to put a napkin in their lap for a meal. Proper use of silverware will come more easily if you all eat together regularly.
- Manners are less important than a pleasant atmosphere, so parents need to balance between teaching and letting things go.
- Young children don't have the attention span to stay at the table for very long, so if they have eaten some dinner and participated a bit in the family discussion, let them be excused. They had a successful time.

Family Focus

At as many meals as possible, the main priority should be sharing some time with the family. The less nagging, the less concern over exactly how much and what someone eats at the meal, and the more time you can all spend relaxing together, the more successful the meal.

The focus of most family discussions is what happened during the day. If kids have trouble volunteering information, try asking about the best thing, the worst thing, or the silliest thing about their day. As children get older, some families ask that the children read an article in the newspaper and come to dinner prepared to discuss it. By age eight, many kids are good enough readers to be able to absorb a short article and prepare to discuss it.

Restaurant Survival

For parents, going to a restaurant offers a break in routine, and before we get there, it always sounds like such a good idea. Whether or not it is a good idea depends largely on how things go with the young set.

Part of growing up involves learning to do things like eat at a restaurant. Unfortunately for Mom and Dad, the learning doesn't always occur smoothly. I've had meals with a baby crawling across my feet while we tried to gulp down a bite or two. I've left restaurants with food spilled here and there. And I have spent a good number of meals following my third daughter around the restaurant—she's never been interested in food—while everyone else in the family sat and tried to finish dinner.

So before you close up this book and decide a meal out is just what the doctor called for, remember that most of the time, a good deal of planning and organization go into making the experience fun for the whole family—including you. Here's how to prepare:

- Take with you the items your young child requires for meals, including bib, special cup, bottle, special seat, and a change of clothing. Also consider packing food, since some kids won't eat restaurant food, or you may need cereal or some snack food to tide them through until the meal comes. Finally, bring a bag with special toys or art supplies. Pack things the kids don't get to use regularly, and select items that are washable and not too valuable. Items get dropped, and it's hard to retrieve everything that falls under the table.
- Select a family-friendly restaurant. This doesn't have to mean fast food. You're generally safe with a Chinese or Italian restaurant, but check out anything called a Sandwich Shoppe. (The extra *pe* on the end may mean it's a delicate little quiet place, better suited to the bridge player crowd.)
- Go early to eat at an off hour.

Did You Know?

Paying attention to what and how you feed kids is increasingly important. The number of overweight youngsters has doubled since the 1960s. One in five American children—20 percent—between the ages of six and seventeen are overweight, putting them at risk for serious illnesses ranging from Type II diabetes and heart disease to asthma.

Trouble Zone!

Restaurant tantrums are relatively common. Kids are tired and hungry, and parental tension can make them stressed. If your child freaks out, take her away from the table and sit with her outside, or even take her to the car and sit with her while she screams it out. Stay with her, holding her and keeping her safe: "We'll go back in the restaurant just as soon as you're ready to follow the restaurant rules again."

- If possible, ask for a table that is off the prime traffic area. If you're in a corner, the kids may be able to get out of their chairs and play quietly in the corner.
- Remove all sharp, breakable, or dangerous items from within reach of your child.
- Don't let the server bring your child's meal first. If that happens, she'll be finished and ready to go when no one else has eaten.
- Speed of service is critical when you're with the family. If you know the menu, some restaurants will take an order over the phone, and it will be ready or almost ready by the time you get there.
- Once you've ordered, walking a child outdoors or around the restaurant will help fill the time.
- Some families make dining out a movable feast. After they have survived the main course at one restaurant, they promise the kids dessert somewhere else. This lessens the time the children have to sit in one spot and generally lets the family conclude with what is more likely to be a successful family dining experience.

If things get tense at the restaurant, you may have to cut your losses and pack up and go.

Mealtimes are a special time for families. By doing what's necessary to create the right atmosphere when your children are young, you'll soon have adolescents who are having such a good time that they are reluctant to leave the family table.

CHAPTER 10

Bedtime

"It's too early for my bath."

"Why do I have to go upstairs now? Rebecca doesn't have to go to bed now."

"I don't want to go to bed yet. I'm not finished with my game."

"I have to give Mommy a great big kiss before I go upstairs."

"I can't get in bed until I tell all the rest of my animals good night."

"One more story, pleeeeeease."

"Where's blankie?" (in an alarmed tone).

"Can I have another drink of water?"

"My eyes won't stay shut."

"Everyone else in my class stays up later than this."

Bedtime is one of those hours when parents are tired, and kids are intent on prolonging the time until you actually leave them alone in their beds. For toddlers, it's one more time when they have to deal with their

Experts say that children resist bedtime for the following reasons:

- They want to declare their independence from your desires.
- They want to stay connected with the parent and not separate for the night.
- They want a sense of control over what is happening to them.
- They want to feel respected and heard.

independence—but this time, instead of actually separating, they'd like to integrate themselves into your night world, too. Older children simply find it more interesting to be up and with you than to be alone and going to sleep, regardless of how tired they may be.

The Importance of the Parental Mind-Set

By evening, it's the rare parent who feels calm and collected. Most of us feel quite frazzled, and bedtime looms as large as a marathon's finish line: "Oh, if only I could get across the line, then I can collapse," we think.

But this is a time to reflect on the fable about the tortoise and the hare. The hare, of course, did himself in by rushing; the tortoise operated at a slow pace with determination. It was, of course, the tortoise who won the race. With your children you'll also find that he who is slow and steady will win the race. Rushing just makes kids anxious, and once they are anxious, they can think of a million and one things to slow you down.

So think of your children's bedtimes as one of your special moments, something you look forward to as an opportunity to enjoy being together. Plan to take a few minutes to help your children wind down. Then, when it's time for lights out, be firm. Eventually, you can establish a pattern of a pleasant bedtime routine followed by a definite hour for leaving your child's room so that you can return to the adult world.

Set a Bedtime Hour and Allow Transition Time

The evening schedule for the family will go much more smoothly if you set a specific bedtime for each of your children. Older children may be able to stay up later than younger ones, but you may be able to link bath times and story times so that one flows into the other one, making it easier for you.

A set evening schedule will aid your children in making the transition. Perhaps they are allowed to watch a thirty-minute television show while you finish the dishes. Or maybe they know they have a certain amount of playtime after dinner before the bedtime routine begins.

Unless the children bathe before dinner, most children need forty-five minutes to an hour for the full routine: bath, story, and bedtime rituals before they can settle down and go to sleep. After all, adults need time for this transition too. Though you may think you go to sleep right away, think back to the moment you start getting ready for bed. It takes most people time to make the transition from the activities of the day to the quiet time of the night. And when we've been out late or don't have time to quiet ourselves down, the quality of our sleep tends to suffer.

Even with a predictable schedule, announce a five-minute warning before it's time to start the bedtime process. To see how this helps, think how violated you would feel if you were downstairs reading a good book and someone came along and forced you to go upstairs, bathe, and get into bed.

Great Idea!

Select which parent is going to be in charge of bedtime. Perhaps you alternate nights, or perhaps each parent is responsible for one child. In some families, one parent does baths, and the other parent takes over for story time.

Establish the Routine

The best routines are ones that allow for some input from the child. Whether it's selecting the books you read or choosing between two pairs of pajamas to sleep in that night, allowing some choice permits children to rise to the occasion and exhibit their best nighttime behavior. The following guidelines can help you establish a peaceful routine:

- Part of the bedtime routine can include selecting an outfit for the next day. This saves time in the morning.
- As you establish what is right for your child, be sure to allow enough time for activities that are important for your child and family. Some children have stuffed animals that need to be put to bed. Some children really enjoy the story time, so be certain this isn't rushed; it's a great opportunity to expose them to so much. Some families sing together as they get closer to bedtime. Some children talk best about their day once the lights are out. If so, turn out the lights a little earlier to allow enough time for listening.
- Don't substitute a television show or a videotape for reading. The animation on the screen is actually quite stimulating, and children who are permitted to watch television before bed have difficulty going to sleep.

At Wit's End

"I can remember what flavor of ice-cream cone my grandmother and I shared at Disney World, but most of the time, I can't remember what day it is. I guess it depends on what you think is important."

—Katherine, age thirteen

- Some children respond well to working with a chart or a checklist for their bedtime activities. Again, it gives them more control.
- Children do best with a night-light in the room. It makes the space seem less frightening.

Especially if your child has difficulty with the bedtime routine, watch for signs of sleep deprivation. A child who isn't getting enough sleep may be cranky, have a short attention span, be restless during the day, and not do well at school.

Sleep needs vary among children, but you can use the following rule of thumb for estimating what your child needs. These times include any naps during the day:

One year old	thirteen and a half hours
Two years old	thirteen hours
Three years old	twelve hours
Five years old	eleven hours
Seven to nine years old	ten to eleven hours
Ten to twelve years old	nine to nine and a half hours

Having a rough idea of your child's sleep needs should help you come up with a workable bedtime, taking into account the hour at which the family gets up.

The Slow-to-Settle

"One more drink," "one more story," "one more kiss"—the list of reasons to keep you can go on interminably. Here's what to do:

- Have your children go to the bathroom right before getting in bed.
- Anticipate the request for water by having a glass of fresh water on the bedside table.
- Allow one (and only one) after-lights-out request. After that, don't come back anymore.
- Music played on a tape recorder in your child's room is a way many people help their child get sleepy.

Trouble Zone!

While most adults feel they could go to sleep instantly the moment their heads hit the pillows, this isn't the case with children. About 25 percent of all children have troublesome sleeping problems. Some have trouble settling down at night, others are early risers, and still others wake in the middle of the night. Frequent night waking is a problem in 20 to 26 percent of one- and two-year-olds, and in 14 percent of three-year-olds. Difficulty in getting in to sleep presents a problem in 15 to 20 percent of one- and two-year-olds and 16 percent of children who are three and older.

- For the child who doesn't want you to leave, offer to come back one more time after he's been in his room five minutes. This gives him five minutes of "getting sleepy" time with the thought that he'll see you one more time before he nods off.
- Be calm but firm. Don't get into power struggles or "five more minutes" and then another "five more minutes," or you're trapped.
- Though little ones can fall asleep more easily if they are held or rocked, this is a poor practice to establish, because children need to be given the gift of being able to soothe themselves to sleep. If your child is sick or going through a night-fear phase, you might stay and rub her back for a few minutes before leaving, but it is best not to feel responsible for seeing that your children are one hundred percent asleep while you are there.

The Night Waker

Whether it's a temporary phase because of nightmares or just your child's sleep pattern, the night waker also needs to have a specific routine for getting back to sleep:

- When he gets up, lead him back to bed. Say simply, "Time for sleep. Good night."

Did You Know?

Early-elementary children who go to bed by 9:00 P.M. handle their stress in a healthier way than their night-owl classmates, and they may outperform them on exams or on the soccer field, suggests a study reported at a recent American Psychosomatic Society annual meeting.

- Some families find that a drink of water, a kiss, and a hug of the child and the teddy bear will do it. If your child is truly afraid, you may need to stay a little longer than for a child who has simply wakened.
- Don't give a bottle or provide a snack, or your children will learn to awaken for this special treat. If you've been giving a bottle with milk or juice, switch to water. Both milk and juice can lead to tooth decay.

The Early Riser

If you have a lark, I can tell you from experience that nothing will change this. My second child is a lark, and she shared a room with her sister. As a baby, she wakened at 3:00 A.M. (then, eventually, at 4:00 A.M. and then 5:00 A.M.), and my husband's and my solution was to bring her into bed with us, where we all slept a little longer. As a teenager, she is still a lark. I am sure we are one of the rare households in America in which the parents are joined by their teen for an early breakfast; not even the sleep habits of adolescence could change her. That said, there are a few things to try so that you can sleep as long as possible:

- Use dark shades to cover the windows. If light is the cause of the early waking, you can do something about that.
- If your child is in a crib, leave safe toys for her to play with, and tell her that's what she's to do when she first wakes up.
- If your child is in a regular bed, she is likely old enough to recognize the position of the hands on a face clock or the numbers on a digital clock. Childproof her room carefully, and leave her with instructions as to what time she can get you.
- For some children, the increased activity in a school day makes them more tired, and they will begin to sleep later.

Like larks, night owls—people who prefer staying up late at night—do not shift sleep habits easily. However, with young children, night owl tendencies do not usually present themselves unless parents are night owls: If you're staying up late, then you may keep your children awake later than other people usually do. While a young night owl may have some difficulty settling down for the night, the under-age-ten set still needs enough sleep that they usually need to go to bed long before parents do. The methods used for the "slow to settle" earlier in this chapter are ones that will help these night birds quiet down. By the time they are teenagers, these kids may stay up much later than you do, but that's a whole different story.

Moving to a Big Bed

Getting a big bed for your child is very exciting, and you need to share his excitement while explaining the rules. "Now that you're in a big bed, you're really growing up. That means you get to sleep in your own bed all night."

Guardrails will protect a child from rolling out of bed and getting hurt, but they won't restrict a child's movements. The first few nights, your child may be giddy with the freedom of being able to get up to come and find you. Be persistent. Keep walking him back to the bedroom and reminding how lucky he is to be able to sleep in a big bed of his own.

The Not-So-Bad Habit

The family bed is a trend that has come back recently. If you are comfortable with allowing the kids in bed with you for part or all of the night, then this is a personal decision. Other families prefer that children have their own beds, but there is sometimes room for some leniency.

A good number of families put the child who isn't feeling well or occasionally is a night waker or early riser into a nest made of a pillow and blankets on the floor of the parents' bedroom. For parents who are comfortable with this arrangement, it can be a nice way of helping them be responsive to the child's needs some of the time without having to spend the night with a four-year-old kicking them in the back periodically.

As you establish a workable system for your children, be consistent. If you are firm and certain in your response to "five minutes more" and "just one more story," you'll save yourself a lot of bedtime bargaining.

Trouble Zone!

You can often avoid parent-child power struggles at bedtime by having a regular routine and an attitude that bedtime is a warm and loving family time. Power struggles and tantrums are never fun, but end-of-the-day ones are certainly the most difficult for all involved.

CHAPTER 11

The School Day and After

Children go to school for a living.

By the time they are in elementary school, they are spending almost seven hours each day in the classrooms, school-yard, and hallways of the school. For children to emerge with the knowledge they need and a strong sense of self-esteem, they need to master three components of this experience:

1. How they manage the day itself
2. How they interact with their peers
3. How they learn to manage their outside responsibilities

Success in all three of these components will maximize your child's success in school.

Getting to School on Time

The child who arrives at school late is off to a bad start. One of the most important jobs you can do as a parent is to establish a schedule that permits your child to get to school on time.

Did You Know?

According to a school psychologist, a good night's sleep and breakfast are two elements that make a huge difference in a child's school day.

- Pack lunches and lay out the next day's clothing the night before. As you've read in other chapters, those activities are best done with help or input from your child. Including your child in decisions about what she'll eat for lunch and what she's willing to wear in the morning will make the process go better.

- Elementary school children and older should pack backpacks the night before. It is also a good idea for them to place their homework in the backpack the moment they have finished it. Running around looking for homework in the morning is a poor behavior for a child to follow.

- Children should dress before breakfast. Get them up early enough that even a preschooler will have time to get dressed. Dressing oneself is easier during the summer months, so if this is a new skill your child is mastering, let her practice during August to prepare for being in charge of herself once school starts.

- Stubbornness may rear its head with the best of children. Humor will often save the day. Offering to race them ("Can you put your socks and shoes on before I'm finished getting dressed?") or being silly ("If you're not going to wear them, I'm going to take your shoes to work with me in my briefcase") can sometimes get you both through a tough morning.

- If a young child is not cooperating, you'll have to take over and help with getting dressed or getting shoes on. "Tomorrow you can do it yourself, but you have to be ready by 8:30." An older child should suffer the consequences of not being ready: if she is late and misses the bus, she walks; if the distance is too great to walk, she goes when one parent is going out anyway.

- Very young children can make their own beds. Use a comforter rather than a blanket and bedspread, and teach your children to sit or stand at the top of the bed to pull up the sheet and comforter. If your children climb out of bed carefully, they need only put the pillow on top to have a decently made bed.

- Checklists can remind children of what they need to do in the morning (get dressed, make bed, comb hair, brush teeth). Use words for school-age children and pictures for little ones.

For ideas about dawdling, see Chapter 8.

Separation Issues

Until your child reaches second grade, you may find yourself dealing with separation issues. Children starting nursery school are young, and leaving a parent is hard for them to do. Kindergarten (new school) and first grade ("Now I'm really going to have to learn something!"), as well as switching schools at any grade, are also daunting in the beginning.

If your child is having difficulty separating, you have a great resource in the classroom teacher. Teachers deal with this issue every year. Also refer to Chapter 4 for ideas about handling clinging and shyness.

Support Your Child's School

Studies show that the most effective schools are those where students, parents, teachers, and administrators help set the rules, and the rules are enforced by all. Even if your school already has a good foundation of rules and standards, the staff doubtless welcomes parent input, and every school appreciates your volunteer time. When children see that you care about their school, they tend to take it more seriously. Here are some basic ways to show support:

- At the beginning of the year, when schools distribute their handbook, read it from cover to cover so that you'll know the school policies, from the vacation schedule to the method for excusing a child for a doctor's appointment. Parents who are disrespectful of the administrative systems put their child in a very peculiar place. Why should children respect the school if their parents clearly don't?
- If there is a separate handbook for students, review it with your children. Otherwise, go through the parents' handbook and read them the relevant parts.
- Make a point of attending all parent functions, and when you can, go on a field trip with the class. Involved parents tend to have children who behave well and enjoy participating in school. If your child is having behavior problems, your presence communicates to her that you care about her, and you'll be able to witness the behavior as it's occurring.

At Wit's End

"In order for children to become successful at the three Rs of reading, 'riting, and 'rithmetic, parents must first teach them the three Rs of respect, responsibility, and resourcefulness. These, not high IQ, define the educable child."

—John Rosemond, family psychologist

Did You Know?

Teachers report that one of the biggest obstacles to helping children is negative attitudes of some of the parents. When called in about a behavior issue, some parents will assume a "not my child's fault" attitude. In that case, teachers have difficulty working with the child. Instead, parents need to arrive at school with an open mind to see what can be done to help their child. The school is on your side, even when there's a problem, because all anyone wants is what is best for the child.

Working with the Teacher

When your child is having trouble socially or academically, take action immediately. Don't wait to get in touch with the teacher. If the issue is bothering you, it may be bothering the teacher, too. Avoid labeling your child, and focus on the specific behaviors that are worrying you. When you meet with the teacher, the two of you can brainstorm ideas that might be helpful. Working together, home and school can accomplish a lot.

If your child is having problems at home (acting out, talking back), then those issues are probably occurring at school, too. If you simply send your child off to school, thinking, "If he misbehaves there, that's their problem," your child is at risk of becoming the kind of child the teacher and staff tend to dislike. By making the teacher your ally, you create a situation where the staff becomes more interested in your child and much more likely to have a vested interest in seeing improvement. Also, teachers are experts at working with all kinds of behaviors, so simply by setting up an initial meeting, you may find answers you had never thought of.

One second-grade teacher supports this point with a story: "The most outrageous excuse I have received was this past year, when I wrote to a mother to express my concern over her son's lack of attentiveness and failure to follow directions or complete any assignments that day. What I hoped for was support from home in the way of an admonition to the child of the importance of paying attention, completing assignments, etc. Instead, I received a note stating the mother was sorry Danny had had a bad day, but that he just wasn't in the mood for school that day! And we wonder why children don't take us seriously."

After School: What to Do When They Crash

When children get home from school, it is not unusual for them to be so worn out that they are irritable or cry over something minor. School and its academic demands are by far the biggest stress for most children. Performance in school is the most public of all their activities. Their own

At Wit's End

Sometimes the "wrongs" that occur at school require no punishment: At one school, the juice containers sold in the cafeteria were not supposed to leave the area. One of the boys tucked the box under his shirt and stuck it in his waistband to sneak it back into the room, where he planned to put it in his backpack to drink later. Unfortunately, the box slipped out of his waistband as he walked down the hall. It broke on the floor, not only alerting the teachers to what had happened but making quite a mess of his pants!

expectations and those of interested adults—parents and teachers—increase the pressure.

Of course, you don't want this type of reaction to be an everyday event for a year. However, you can expect this type of behavior at the start of a school year, after an illness, or when family stress is high. Sometimes children can't wait until they are home, and they act out while still at school. Both situations are caused by bad feelings—pent-up ones or otherwise.

Children need to be able to cry and work through their feelings. During the school day, they meet with countless challenges and disappointments, and they need to express their feelings. In general, if you let your child vent for a little bit and listen sympathetically, he'll regain his energy and be off to do something fun before the afternoon is too old.

As kids get older, it becomes less acceptable to cry. Even so, they generally find some way to express that they are upset. For boys, this feeling may be expressed by withdrawing, so you need to be tuned in. Ask them if something is bothering them and listen to anything they may say.

If your child is getting upset at school, check with your teacher so the two of you can figure out what is wrong. Is the academic part of the day stressful? Is your child having trouble socially? If your child knows you are concerned when things aren't going well, she'll already

be bolstered by that support. The underlying message should always be, "If something is bothering you at school, what can we do to help you out?"

School-Yard Bullies

The National School Safety Center estimates that 2.5 million American schoolchildren are bullied, intimidated, or victimized daily. Nearly 80 percent of all schoolchildren report that they are being bullied at one time or another. An estimated 160,000 American children fail to attend school each day because they are afraid of attack or intimidation by other students.

This is no minor problem. Talk to your school about establishing an antibullying campaign that raises awareness and presents intervention methods to reduce the level of bullying in our schools. For more specific information, see Chapter 6, "Aggressive Behavior and Bullying."

Play Dates That Work

One of the best ways to help your preschool and early elementary child adjust to school each year is to set up play dates with other kids in the classroom. When young children have a new friend visiting for the first time, you need to plan to supervise carefully. Elementary school children will do a bit better, but if the other child has never been to your home, stay within earshot in case the kids start having difficulty. Here are some guidelines for planning a successful play date:

- Before any invitation is extended by either parent or child, sound out your child about whom to invite. The child's mother may be the nicest person in the world, but if your child has taken a dislike to her child, the play date isn't going to work.
- Three really is a crowd. Try to keep play dates restricted to inviting one friend at at time. Threesomes inevitably break down to two against one, and that's never fun for anyone.

- After a school day (even if it's only a morning for the preschool set), keep it short. With little ones, sometimes an hour will seem like a very long time to both of you. You may even want to suggest the parent or caregiver come along so that the other child feels comfortable at your house.

- Discuss with your child some of the things he might want to do with the friend. TV and computer games are poor ideas, because they don't permit as much socializing as some other activities do. Also, discuss whether there are any toys that ought to be put away (not to be shared) before a friend arrives. Even elementary school children may have special toys like a model plane or doll collection that they feel very possessive of. Because everything else will be shared, it's fine for a child of any age to stipulate that certain things should be put away for the event.

- Stay nearby while the play date is getting under way. The children may need some suggestions from you as they decide what they want to do.

- If possible, keep younger siblings occupied with other activities. Although letting both kids have play dates on the same day can be a bit hectic, it can distract the younger one so the older kids have an opportunity to socialize with each other.

- Plan for some break time. Lunch or a healthful snack may provide the breather the kids need. Also think about what your own child does to unwind. Whether it's an art project, music, or a book you can read with them, have a backup plan in case things aren't going that well.

- If the play date seems to be deteriorating, don't jump in immediately. See if the kids can work out their problems themselves. Sometimes you may have to explain house rules to a guest if his behavior is causing a problem.

- If a conflict becomes verbally or physically combative, intervene and be firm about what you expect. Stop the negative behavior and then talk with the children about finding a compromise. If they cannot settle their differences with the game at hand, suggest something else for them to do, even if it involves coming to the kitchen to help you.

Great Idea!

Cleanup is a responsibility of playing together. Work with both children on putting things away. (This may be an eye-opener to some children, but that's OK. They'll be cleaning up at school, even if they aren't made to do so at home.)

- Give a five-minute warning to cleanup time to help children make the transition to the time when the friend must go home.
- If the kids have made anything, be sure the guest takes her project home.
- If your child has difficulty with good-byes, consider leaving the house at the same time the friend and her parent do. You can walk partway home with them or go to the store—something that helps your child deal with the transition better than lying on the floor and being resent-ful or angry that the play date is over.
- When a play date goes well, praise your child and his friend.

Homework Habits That Last a Lifetime

Family stress over homework is legendary. Whether you're encouraging an overtired first-grader to take "just one more look" at the addition prob-lems or demanding that your eleven-year-old turn off the television until after her schoolwork is done, supervising homework can be very time-consuming for parents.

If you establish a specific homework routine for your children, the entire family will benefit. You'll save time, and your efforts will help instill in your children productive work habits and an organized approach to problem solving.

Whether their homework is to bring in a leaf or to solve twenty math problems, children will carry throughout their lifetime the habits they establish while doing school assignments.

The Space
Set up a work area for your child, keeping in mind these features:

- *Central location (for a young child)*—A table or desk in the family room or kitchen is ideal for the homework novice, because it's easier for an adult to provide help and encouragement. Be careful that the location you choose doesn't have too many distractions. You may also want to buy a desk for your child; it provides storage and will be used later on.
- *Decent lighting*—Consider whether the child is left- or right-handed when evaluating the light.

- *Child-friendly chair*—Be certain your child is comfortable in the chair she uses. A footstool for the feet of younger children can make a normal kitchen chair more comfortable. If your child is a floor sprawler and does her homework well, don't tamper with her method.

The Supplies

Remember the excitement of new school supplies? You can kindle enthusiasm for school by stocking a "homework office." In addition to all the school basics (pencils, pens, markers, notebooks, stapler, glue), also have the following useful items on hand:

- *Calendar*—As soon as the school sends out the calendar with dates for vacation and special events, help your child mark these on his or her calendar.
- *Assignment notebook (something small, perhaps three by five inches)*—Particularly if the teacher has no organized method for giving assignments, teach your child to write down assignments in a notebook so that everything to be done will be listed in one place. Set up each page to record the date, assignment, due date, and the date the assignment was handed in.
- *Folders for homework*—Teach organizational skills early. By putting paperwork for each class in its own folder, your child can avoid having to rummage through all of his things for that field-trip permission slip he needs.
- *Storage file*—Use an accordion-style file folder with dividers for keeping schoolwork that has been graded and returned. Label the folder with your child's name and school year.
- *Two dictionaries, one children's and one adult's*—The children's dictionary is valuable for its simplicity and pictures. But kids often ask about words that aren't listed in a children's dictionary, so the adult dictionary is necessary, even for young children.
- *Atlas*—An atlas is a great reference for the whole family.
- *Poster board*—Keep five or six pieces on hand for making the often-assigned poster.
- *Twenty to thirty old magazines*—Keep magazines on hand for creating collages and for other assignments. Nature magazines are best for this purpose.

At Wit's End

One teacher reported that one of her brighter ten-year-old students was quite angry about having to copy information down from the blackboard. To "get even," he wrote the whole thing backward so that it could be read from the back if you shone a light on the front of the page. "He learned far more about himself and that particular homework assignment than I ever intended!" she chuckled.

Visit an office supply store and purchase some organizing aids to store items neatly. You can keep the smaller items in a school supplies box or a desk-size carousel. The larger items should be on the child's desk. If your child will be working in the family room or kitchen, make space for supplies on a nearby shelf, or use a rolling cart so everything will be close at hand.

Your Role in the Process

Almost all schools have a back-to-school night early in the year. At this meeting, find out the answers to the following questions:

- How will assignments come home?
- How much time is your child expected to spend on homework each night?
- What is the parent's role in the process? Should parents point out errors and see that the child corrects them?
- What is the best way to contact the teacher if your child is having difficulty with homework?

The Nightly Schedule

Homework time should be structured and specific. Here are some ideas for establishing and enforcing a schedule:

- Some children prefer to get their homework done right after school, but most kids like to relax first. Establish the best time according to your child's needs—preferably before dinner!
- For children who have difficulty sitting still, establish break times. Set a timer for fifteen minutes of work time, then a five-minute break. Keep resetting the time until the homework is completed.
- Don't interrupt your child during homework. Phone calls can be returned later, and if your child forgot to do his morning chores, discuss it with him *after* he finishes his homework.
- If possible, plan to set a quiet tone by doing some work of your own (paying bills, writing letters, going over your own office tasks) while your child works.

- On the days your child has no homework, maintain the routine by encouraging your child to use the time for reading. (Still, there's nothing nicer than an occasional day off!)

Getting It Done

For children eight and younger, you, an older sibling, or a capable sitter need to be nearby in case help is needed. Here are some specific ways to help a child of any age:

- To begin, review the assignments, and suggest that your child start by doing the most difficult one first. Ask your child to explain how he is going to proceed.
- If the assignment is to write a story or an essay, teach her to begin by talking it through. This helps clarify where the story is going, what ending will be best, and any kind of twist that needs to be included.
- Teach a child to skip difficult problems and come back to them. Later, if a problem is still too difficult, he can ask for help.
- Teach your child to break a long-term assignment into parts. Help your child assess the steps involved. For example, a research report might include the following steps:

  1. Select a topic.
  2. Get the teacher's approval.
  3. Visit the library and look for books.
  4. Go on the Internet and search the subject.
  5. Read and digest material.
  4. Write a first draft of the report.
  5. Prepare cover.
  6. Revise and print final draft.

  Together, agree on personal due dates for each step, then put them on the calendar.
- Teach children the benefits of completing work early. Encourage your child to work on major projects at a steady pace, setting a personal completion date a day or so before the teacher's due date. This will help your child establish a positive, lifelong pattern for meeting deadlines.

- Teach older children how to use their textbooks effectively. Demonstrate how to preview a book, checking the table of contents and examining what reference information is available. Are there maps? Is there a glossary? Any appendixes?
- Help a child set reasonable goals. If your child is getting only four out of ten spelling words correct, she needs to focus on getting five right the next time, not getting a perfect score. Create a chart that shows how she is progressing. Using the chart, you can show her she can improve from five right to six right, rather than either of you aspiring to an instant jump to a perfect ten.
- Make sure your child places completed homework in his backpack as soon as he has finished it. Monitor this practice until you're certain it has become second nature.

By helping your child adapt nicely to the school day and expressing your own interest in learning, you'll have taken an important step toward helping your child enjoy school. And that's nine-tenths of the battle of being a good student.

CHAPTER 12

What to Do if You're Still Puzzled

If you've worked your way through this book and your child is still having difficulties, then there are three questions to consider:

1. Is it stress?
2. Does your child do better with one parent than another?
3. Should you consult a professional?

Stress and Your Child

Like adults, children worry, and they think about things that worry them—their family situation, their performance in school, their friends (or lack of them), and major world events. For many children, their plate is overly full of worries, and this creates bad behavior. Here are some things you can do:

- Children need to be encouraged to talk about what is bothering them. That alone is a good stress reliever.
- Remember the power of exercise. After your children have spent a long day being cooped up at school, send them outside to play for a little while. They'll feel a lot better for having burned off excess energy.
- Spend quality time together doing something fun. That's good for everybody.

At Wit's End

"The more I encourage a child to think for himself, the more he will care what I think."

—Anonymous

- As children get a little older (that is, kindergarten and up), consider teaching them relaxation exercises. Teach your child the following techniques:
  - Lie down and think about tightening and relaxing every part of your body. Start by tightening and releasing the toes, then move your way up to the feet, ankles, legs, buttocks, and so on until as many parts of the body as you can think of have been put through this relaxation process.
  - Imagine yourself in a peaceful setting. For a child, this might be thinking of himself lying on a warm beach or by a pool or even just lying on his own bed. Your child may surprise you with the peaceful places he thinks of!
  - Sit in a chair. Put a hand on your chest. Pretend your body is a building, and with the first breath in, fill only the upper floors. Begin filling your body with air lower and lower until you breathe in to get air all the way into the basement. In the process, the breathing slows down, and you'll feel calmer.

  The more relaxation techniques you can teach your children, the better prepared they will be for coping in the adult world.
- Consider yoga classes for your child. All aspects of yoga, from breathing techniques to body stretching, are good for children and adults.

Is It You—or Your Spouse?

Often children behave better for one adult than another. If you're beside yourself because of your child's behavior, give yourself a break. It will help you and your child, too.

If your child consistently misbehaves when you're around, put your spouse or caregiver in charge of those times when your child is giving you a tough time. That adult will likely receive better behavior, and this permits you to cool down for a few days.

During this cooldown period, spend positive time with your child. What do the two of you like to do together? If you're not sure, ask your child. By mending the relationship with some positive interactions, you'll be able to work back to the point where you can give the baths or handle bedtime. Sometimes you both just need a vacation.

Consulting a Professional

The first professionals you consult should be those who know your child best—the teacher and perhaps the principal or school psychologist. Describe the behavior that is of concern to you, and ask the person's opinion as to what you should do.

The next person to talk to should be your child's doctor. Pediatricians are knowledgeable about normal and age-appropriate behaviors, even if they have never observed your child acting out.

The professionals you speak to may be reassuring, telling you to give the problem more time. Or they may have suggestions about other professionals who can offer advice.

Of course, when behavior problems become a big issue, parents worry about different conditions they have heard of. Only a professional can offer you an accurate diagnosis, but for your convenience, here are brief definitions of some terms you may have heard:

- *Attention deficit/hyperactivity disorder (ADHD)*—This is one everyone has heard of. Children who are diagnosed with ADHD have difficulty sitting still and paying attention. The behavior can range from fidgeting to an inability to stay seated—and sometimes problems with staying in bed at night. These children are easily distracted, and it affects their ability to interact with others as well as to do well in school.
- *Adjustment disorder*—This is a fancy way of saying that a child is having trouble adjusting to a major stressor in her life. To qualify as an adjustment disorder, the problem needs to have created difficulties for three months or longer from the time of the stressful occurrence. Children with adjustment disorder may withdraw from friends and activities, do less well in school, and worry excessively.
- *Conduct disorder*—Children with this disorder show a chronic pattern (six months or more) of either violating age-appropriate rules or violating the rights of others by bullying, lying, or initiating negative behavior toward other people or animals.
- *Generalized anxiety disorder*—Anxiety is a normal emotion that aids in survival, but sometimes children become overly stressed and worry so much that they have physiological symptoms such as headaches,

Great Idea!

Compliments do wonders to improve a child's behavior, so if you've run into a difficult time with your child, try to find things he is doing well, and praise him. It will help behavior and also self-esteem, which is probably at a low.

Great Idea!

Part of reducing stress for your child is bringing your own stress level down, so here's some wonderful advice: When you're really feeling under pressure, do whatever helps you unwind. Tell your children, "I need a minute to calm down." Don't be angry with yourself. You're setting a great example!

stomachaches, difficulty sleeping, restlessness, and difficulty concentrating.

- *Oppositional defiant disorder*—A child who acts belligerent for six months or longer may be diagnosed with this condition. The behavior may involve losing his temper, arguing with adults, refusing to follow rules, purposely annoying people, blaming others, being easily irritated, being spiteful, or getting angry frequently.

- *Obsessive compulsive disorder (OCD)*—This disorder consists of two types of behavior: obsessions and compulsions. Obsessions are recurrent and persistent worries that are not realistic or typical. For example, a child might fear germs and worry about picking them up from touching doorknobs and stair rails. Compulsions are repetitive actions that the person uses to drive away the obsessive thoughts. Repetitive handwashing is the classic example of OCD. Compulsive actions may take hours each day to perform. A child may show either obsessions or compulsions, though they often go together.

- *Phobias*—A phobia is an intense fear reaction to a specific object or situation. Young children can have phobias about a good number of things. If the phobia is severe, professional help can make a big difference in your child's life.

- *Pica*—A person with this disorder eats inedible substances or objects such as hair, dirt, rocks, plaster, leaves, paper, or even feces. Ingesting these substances can cause intestinal problems and can be quite serious. While toddlers go through a phase of putting many things in their mouths, children who are diagnosed with pica are children who continue this behavior after they are toddlers. Sometimes pica is caused by a vitamin or mineral deficiency.

- *Post-traumatic stress disorder (PTSD)*—If your child has suffered a particular trauma, from a dog attack to an unpleasant breakup of your marriage, it is not unusual for this to result in PTSD. Again, children can be helped if you connect them with a professional.

- *Selective mutism*—Children with this disorder refuse to speak in certain situations. The most commonly noticed form of selective mutism occurs in children who otherwise seem normal but refuse to speak in school.

- *Sleep disorders*—Whether a child is getting too much or too little sleep, she may feel tired and lethargic, and life is just generally difficult for these children. Three notable disorders are insomnia, hypersomnia, and narcolepsy.

- *Insomnia*—Children with insomnia have trouble going to sleep or staying asleep.
- *Hypersomnia*—A child with hypersomnia sleeps too much or naps often during the day; the problem must continue for longer than a month before it is diagnosed as this disorder.
- *Narcolepsy*—Narcolepsy causes a person to fall asleep suddenly and unexpectedly. This condition must persist for at least three months before it can be diagnosed as such. It is not particularly common in children.

- *Speech problems*—A child who has a problem with oral expression or communication issues may have any of a number of speech disorders. Most schools have speech therapists on staff who do evaluations in the early grades so that these disorders can be diagnosed and treated with therapy as early as possible.
  - *Expressive language disorder*—These children are not able to speak as well as they can think.
  - *Mixed receptive-expressive language disorder*—These kids have difficulty speaking as well as understanding what is said.
  - *Phonological disorder*—Youngsters with this disorder have difficulty pronouncing particular sounds; this is very common in young children.
  - *Stuttering*—Kids who stutter repeat certain sounds and syllables and have difficulty controlling their stuttering.
- *Tics*—These are involuntary rapid movements that appear abnormal but may not have a medical cause. Some tics, such as eye twitches or blinking or jerking of the head, involve motor control. Others are vocal, such as coughing, repeating certain phrases, or repeating what others say.

A professional can help you with any of these conditions. Sometimes medication is needed, but often the doctor can provide a family with behavioral methods that will help their child get through a tough time.

Though some people think children "have it easy," childhood is a time of great change that brings with it a fair degree of stress. If you ever have any concerns that your child is having an excessive amount of difficulty—or you feel you need more information in order to help—don't hesitate to contact your child's teacher, a school administrator, or your pediatrician. Simply talking out what your concerns are may be very helpful, and in turn, you'll be better prepared to help your child.

Parenting is the most difficult—and potentially the most rewarding—job you may ever undertake. To start with this less-than-ten-pound being and to have the honor of raising him or her all the way to adulthood is a very large responsibility. With hard work and good humor, you will find that one of parenting's best rewards is a child who behaves well and enjoys being with you.

Resources

The following resources may be helpful to you if you want to learn more about some of the topics covered in this book.

Websites

www.addhelpline.org
This site is dedicated to providing information and support for parents and teachers who are involved with children with attention deficit disorder.

www.antibullying.net
This website offers a resource for children, parents, and teachers who are looking for advice about doing away with bullying.

www.bullying.org
Here, young people will find stories, poems, songs, and film clips that help them through a time when they may feel they are being victimized by a bully.

http://npin.org
This site is run by the National Parent Information Network and features parenting news and a complete archive of articles on various parenting topics with a special focus on family involvement in education.

www.parenting.com

This *Parenting* magazine site offers all the resources of the magazine, from helpful articles to ratings on toys and advice on giving birthday parties.

www.parenting.org

The information on this site is compiled by a team of professionals at the Girls and Boys Town National Resource and Training Center. Their mission is to provide advice on "day-to-day care taking, guidance, and development of your child."

www.parentingresources.ncjrs.org

This site is federally sponsored through the Coordinating Council on Juvenile Justice and Delinquency Prevention and addresses topics that include school violence, child development, homeschooling, organized sports, child abuse, and the juvenile justice system.

www.parentstages.com

This site provides information for parents as their children go through various stages, and covers everything from health issues to financial matters.

www.positiveparenting.com

This site offers an E-mail newsletter and information on parenting and recommends books on parenting. The information is aimed at both parents and teachers.

www.shykids.com

Support and information for kids, parents, and teachers on what it feels like to be shy—and how to overcome it—are the ingredients of this website.

www.tnpc.com

This site, sponsored by the National Parenting Center, features *ParenTalk* newsletter and numerous articles about all aspects of parenting, from learning issues to behavioral ones.

Chat Groups

Various service providers such as Yahoo and AOL sponsor chat groups that parents can join. Check what is available through your service and find out if this Internet replacement for neighbor-to-neighbor advice works for you.

Organizations

Coalition for Children, Inc.

This organization provides community-based and school-based information to educate parents, teachers, and children regarding child abuse, bullying, and other issues involving children's safety. Contact them at www.safechild.org; Sherryll Kraizer, Ph.D., Executive Director, Coalition for Children, Inc., P.O. Box 6304, Denver, CO 80206; phone: 303-320-6321; fax: 303-320-6328.

International MOMS Club

This organization supports mothers who choose to stay home with their children instead of working outside the household. There are chapters all across the country. Contact them at www.momsclub.org; MOMS Club, 25371 Rye Canyon Road, Valencia, CA 91355.

National Parent Teacher Association

Almost every school has a PTA chapter. However, for parents who have an issue they would like to explore on a nationwide basis, contact them at www.pta.org; 330 North Wabash Avenue, Suite 2100, Chicago, IL 60611; phone: 312-670-6782; toll-free phone: 800-307-4782; fax: 312-670-6703.

The Parent Institute

This organization is dedicated to encouraging parents to become involved in their children's education. They offer newsletters, booklets, and videos on that subject. Contact them at www.parent-institute.com; P.O. Box 7474, Fairfax Station, VA 22039-7474; phone: 703-323-9170; toll-free phone: 800-756-5525; fax: 800-216-3667.

Parents Leadership Institute

The website for this organization has a complete list of articles on everything from biting to time management for parents. The organization is dedicated to helping parents deal with simple issues, such as improving listening skills, and more complex ones, such as racism and poverty. Contact them at www.parentleaders.org; P.O. Box 50492, Palo Alto, CA 94303; phone: 650-322-LEAD; fax: 650-322-5179.

Parents Without Partners, Inc.

This international organization is dedicated to providing support and information for parents who are bringing up children on their own. Contact them at www.parentswithoutpartners.org; 1650 South Dixie Highway, Suite 510, Boca Raton, FL 33432; phone: 561-391-8833.

Index